OXFORD
Primary
ATLAS

Editorial Adviser
Dr Patrick Wiegand

OXFORD
UNIVERSITY PRESS

Great Clarendon Street, Oxford OX2 6DP

Oxford University Press is a department of the University of Oxford.
It furthers the University's objective of excellence in research, scholarship,
and education by publishing worldwide in

Oxford   New York

Auckland   Cape Town   Dar es Salaam   Hong Kong   Karachi
Kuala Lumpur   Madrid   Melbourne   Mexico City   Nairobi
New Delhi   Shanghai   Taipei   Toronto

With offices in

Argentina   Austria   Brazil   Chile   Czech Republic   France   Greece
Guatemala   Hungary   Italy   Japan   Poland   Portugal   Singapore
South Korea   Switzerland   Thailand   Turkey   Ukraine   Vietnam

Oxford is a registered trade mark of Oxford University Press
in the UK and in certain other countries

ISBN-13: 978 0 19 832160 6 (hardback)
ISBN-10: 0 19 832160 0 (hardback)

ISBN-13: 978 0 19 832159 0 (paperback)
ISBN-10: 0 19 832159 7 (paperback)

7 9 10 8 6

Printed in Singapore

Acknowledgements

Illustrations by:
Julian Baker p 20; Adrian Barclay pp 31, 35, 41, 51, 54, 55; Mark Duffin pp 7 (compass), 23tl, tr & br, 24 (bricks), 26, 59; Nick Hawken pp 24 (settlements), 32, 33, 36, 37, 38, 39, 42, 43, 45, 46, 47, 48, 49, 52, 53, 55; Tracey Learoyd and Adrian Smith p 20 *and thereafter* (landscape pictograms); ODI p 24 *and thereafter* (population figures); Harry Venning p 60

The publishers would also like to thank the following for permission to reproduce the following photographs:
Alamy pp 20t (Robert Harding Picture Library), 20ct (The Photolibrary Wales), 20c (Geogphotos), 20cb (Worldwide Picture Library), 22tr (Leslie Garland Picture Library), 24t (David Crausby), 24c (Elmtree Images), 26t (David Martyn Hughes), 26b (Gina Calvi), 29ct (Jon Arnold Images), 29cb (Ian Thraves), 39t (Robert Harding Picture Library), 48t (ImageState), 60cr (Steve Bloom Images), 60l (TH Foto), 60r (Guy Somerset), 64tc (Robert Harding Picture Library), 64bl (ashfordplatt); Corbis pp 20b (Chinch Gryniewicz), 22tl (David Paterson), 23tl (Neil Beer), 26c (Jason Hawkes), 28t (Martin Jones), 33b (ML Sinibaldi), 36t (Lindsay Hebberd), 36b (Richard Bickel), 42br (Charles Lenars), 52t (Jeremy Horner), 64tr (Ron Watts), 65tr (Richard A. Cooke), 65bc (Galen Rowell), 65bl (Wolfgang Kaehler); Frank Lane Picture Agency pp 29b (Chris Demetriou), 42br (Derek Hall), 43ct (Peter Davey), 43br (David Hosking), 64tl (Minden Pictures); Getty Images/Photographer's Choice p 46l

(James Randklev); Getty Images/Stone pp 24b (Patrick Ingrand), 29tr (Tony Page), 33t, 42t (Will & Deni McIntyre), 43l (Daryl Balfour), 46r, 52b (Pascal Rondeau), 58br; Getty Taxi pp 28b (Richard Cooke), 39b, 47r (B & M Productions), 48b (Tom Bean); Getty Images/The Image Bank pp 47l, 58bl (Image Makers), 64br, 65tl, 65br (Frans Lemmens); Heritage Image Partnership © The British Museum p 28ct (Institution Reference: M&ME, 1939,10-10,93); Powerstock p 28cb (Superstock); Science Photo Library pp 8 (NRSC Ltd), 59l (Earth Satellite Corporation), 59r (Planetary Visions Ltd), 60cl (David Vaughan); © UK Perspectives p 27.

The page design is by Adrian Smith.

The publishers are grateful to the following colleagues in geography education for their helpful comments and advice during the development stages of this atlas:

Jeremy Bullock, Susan Butler, Claire Condie, John Dewis, Tracey Ellis, John Halocha, Joan Huckle, Richard Jefferies, Pat Kelway, Amanda Lightfoot, Trevor Mason, Vanessa Richards, Vicky Stevenson, Emma Wells, Niki Whitburn, Brenda Whittle.

The publishers would also like to thank Phoenix Mapping and Suzanne Williams for their help during the production of this atlas.

2 Contents

The United Kingdom

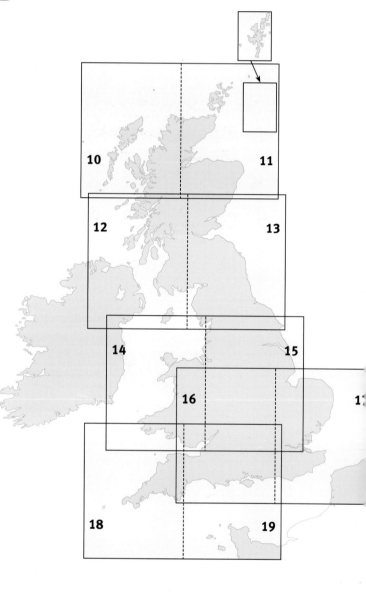

DATE DUE

US 23

PRINTED IN U.S.A.

World Flags

 Afghanistan
 Albania
 Algeria
 Andorra
 Angola
 Antigua and Barbuda
 Argentina

 Armenia
 Australia
 Austria
 Azerbaijan
 Bahamas
 Bahrain
 Bangladesh

 Barbados
 Belarus
 Belgium
 Belize
 Benin
 Bhutan
 Bolivia

 Bosnia-Herzegovina
 Botswana
 Brazil
 Brunei
 Bulgaria
 Burkina
 Burundi

 Cambodia
 Cameroon
 Canada
 Cape Verde
 Central African Republic
 Chad
 Chile

 China
 Colombia
 Comoros
 Congo
 Congo, Dem. Rep.
 Costa Rica
 Côte d'Ivoire

 Croatia
 Cuba
 Cyprus
 Czech Republic
 Denmark
 Djibouti
 Dominica

 Dominican Republic
 East Timor
 Ecuador
 Egypt
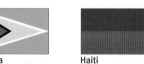 El Salvador
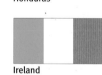 Equatorial Guinea
 Eritrea

 Estonia
 Ethiopia
 Fiji
 Finland
 France
 French Guiana
 Gabon

Gambia
 Georgia
Germany
 Ghana
Greece
Greenland
 Grenada

 Guatemala
Guinea
 Guinea-Bissau
Guyana
Haiti
Honduras
Hungary

Iceland
India
Indonesia
Iran
Iraq
Ireland
Israel

Italy
 Jamaica
Japan
Jordan
Kazakhstan
Kenya
Kiribati

Kuwait
Kyrgyzstan
Laos
Latvia
Lebanon
Lesotho
Liberia

Flags World

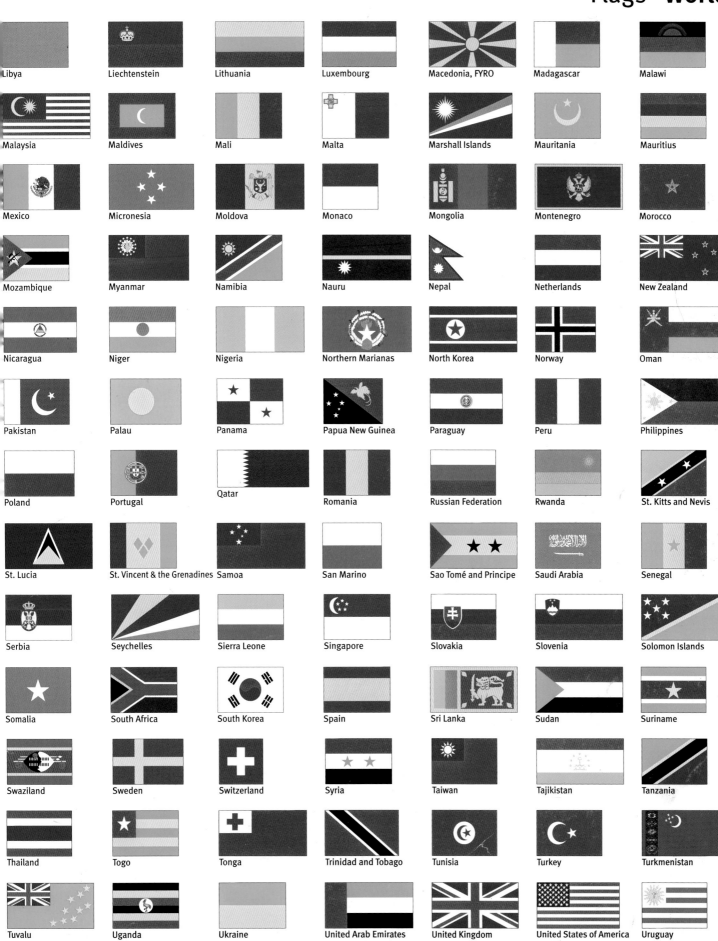

Libya	Liechtenstein	Lithuania	Luxembourg	Macedonia, FYRO	Madagascar	Malawi
Malaysia	Maldives	Mali	Malta	Marshall Islands	Mauritania	Mauritius
Mexico	Micronesia	Moldova	Monaco	Mongolia	Montenegro	Morocco
Mozambique	Myanmar	Namibia	Nauru	Nepal	Netherlands	New Zealand
Nicaragua	Niger	Nigeria	Northern Marianas	North Korea	Norway	Oman
Pakistan	Palau	Panama	Papua New Guinea	Paraguay	Peru	Philippines
Poland	Portugal	Qatar	Romania	Russian Federation	Rwanda	St. Kitts and Nevis
St. Lucia	St. Vincent & the Grenadines	Samoa	San Marino	Sao Tomé and Principe	Saudi Arabia	Senegal
Serbia	Seychelles	Sierra Leone	Singapore	Slovakia	Slovenia	Solomon Islands
Somalia	South Africa	South Korea	Spain	Sri Lanka	Sudan	Suriname
Swaziland	Sweden	Switzerland	Syria	Taiwan	Tajikistan	Tanzania
Thailand	Togo	Tonga	Trinidad and Tobago	Tunisia	Turkey	Turkmenistan
Tuvalu	Uganda	Ukraine	United Arab Emirates	United Kingdom	United States of America	Uruguay
Uzbekistan	Vanuatu	Venezuela	Vietnam	Yemen	Zambia	Zimbabwe

Contents 3

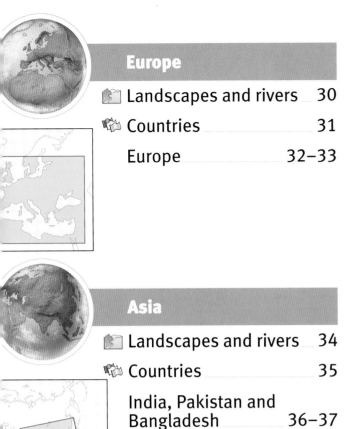

4 Atlas literacy

Map language

There are special names for the parts of maps

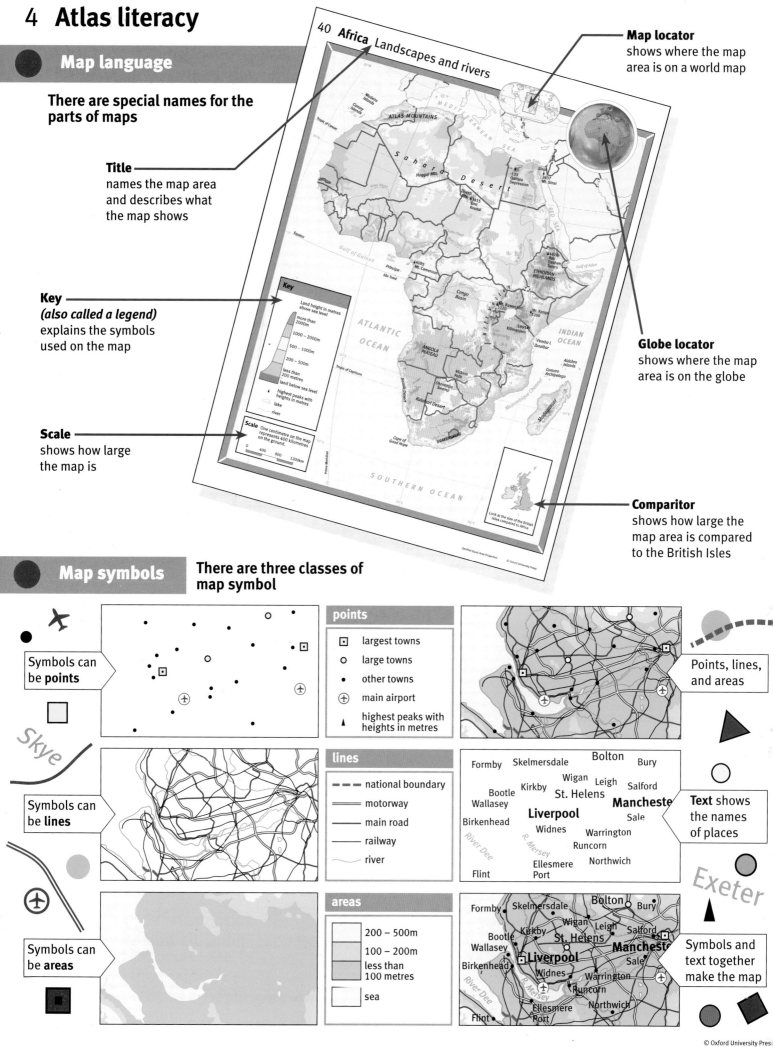

Title
names the map area and describes what the map shows

Key
(also called a legend)
explains the symbols used on the map

Scale
shows how large the map is

Map locator
shows where the map area is on a world map

Globe locator
shows where the map area is on the globe

Comparitor
shows how large the map area is compared to the British Isles

Map symbols

There are three classes of map symbol

Symbols can be **points**

Symbols can be **lines**

Symbols can be **areas**

points
- ⊡ largest towns
- ○ large towns
- • other towns
- ⊕ main airport
- ▲ highest peaks with heights in metres

lines
- – – – national boundary
- ═══ motorway
- ─── main road
- ─── railway
- ～～ river

areas
- 200 – 500m
- 100 – 200m
- less than 100 metres
- sea

Points, lines, and areas

Text shows the names of places

Symbols and text together make the map

Type on maps

The way text is printed on maps gives an important clue to what the words mean

Great Britain *Ireland*	islands
UNITED KINGDOM **REPUBLIC OF IRELAND**	countries
ENGLAND **SCOTLAND** **WALES** **NORTHERN IRELAND**	parts of the United Kingdom
PENNINES *GRAMPIAN MOUNTAINS*	physical features
Ben Nevis Snowdon	mountain peaks
NORTH SEA *English Channel*	sea areas
Manchester York Dover	settlements

Map abbreviations

An abbreviation is a shortened version of a word or a group of words

Some country names are abbreviated using the first letters of each word

R.	River
Mt.	Mount
Is.	Island
Pen.	Peninsula

UK   United Kingdom

USA   United States of America

UAE   United Arab Emirates

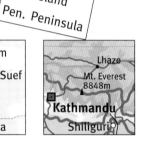

Country names and adjectives

There are patterns in the way some country names make adjectives

Australia	*Australian*	Ireland	*Irish*
India	*Indian*	Poland	*Polish*
Nigeria	*Nigerian*	Sweden	*Swedish*
Zambia	*Zambian*	Turkey	*Turkish*
China	*Chinese*	Brazil	*Brazilian*
Japan	*Japanese*	Canada	*Canadian*
Malta	*Maltese*	Egypt	*Egyptian*
Taiwan	*Taiwanese*	Italy	*Italian*
		Bangladesh	*Bangladeshi*
		Iraq	*Iraqi*
		Israel	*Israeli*
		Pakistan	*Pakistani*

Other country names make adjectives with no pattern

Cyprus	*Cypriot*	Greece	*Greek*	Peru	*Peruvian*
France	*French*	Iceland	*Icelandic*	Slovakia	*Slovak*
Germany	*German*	Netherlands	*Dutch*	Thailand	*Thai*

Map punctuation

A country name in brackets shows that a place is part of that country

Corsica is part of France

The Bulgarian *flag*

The Danish *flag*

The Argentinian *flag*

The Senegalese *flag*

6 Atlas numeracy

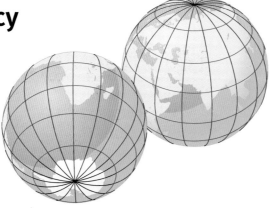

The Earth is a sphere*.

Two sets of imaginary lines help us describe where places are on the Earth.

All the lines are numbered and some have special names.

* It's actually slightly flattened at the north and south poles.

Longitude

Lines of longitude measure distance east or west of the Prime Meridian.

The **Prime Meridian** (also called the Greenwich Meridian) is at longitude 0°.

The **International Date Line** (on the other side of the Earth) is based on longitude 180°.

Latitude

Lines of latitude measure distance north or south of the equator.

The equator is at latitude 0°.

The poles are at latitude 90°N and 90°S.

Arctic Circle
60°N
40°N
Tropic of Cancer
20°N
0° Equator
20°S
Tropic of Capricorn
40°S
60°S
Antarctic Circle

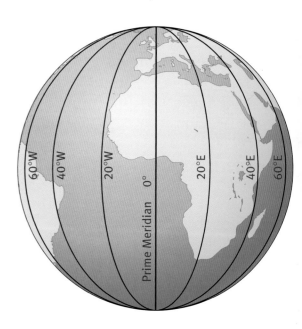

60°W 40°W 20°W 0° 20°E 40°E 60°E
Prime Meridian

Map projections

There are many ways of showing the Earth on a flat map.

World map used in the United Kingdom and Europe

World map used in Australia and New Zealand

Grid codes

In this atlas, the lines of latitude and longitude are used to make a grid.

The columns of the grid have letters.

The rows of the grid have numbers.

Numbers and letters together make a grid code that can be used to describe where places are on the Earth.

Abuja is in B4   Durban is in C2

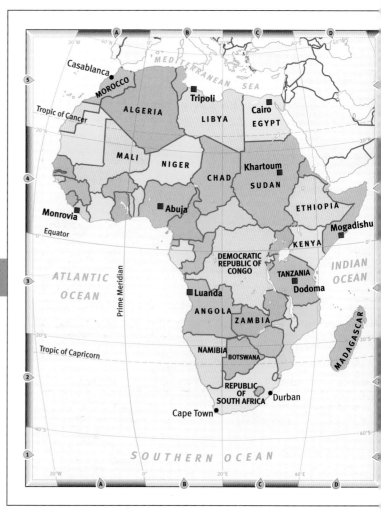

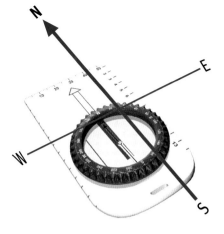

Direction

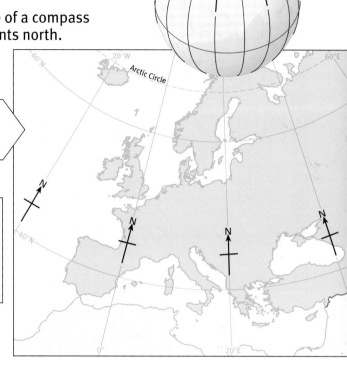

A compass is used for finding direction.

The needle of a compass always points north.

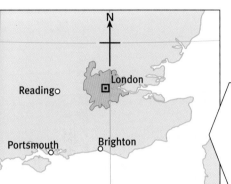

North on atlas maps follows the lines of longitude.

London is north of Brighton.

Brighton is south of London.

Reading is west of London.

Portsmouth is south west of London.

Scale

Maps are much, much smaller than the countries they show.

A few centimetres on the map stand for very many kilometres on the ground.

Each division on the scale line is one centimetre. The scale line shows how many kilometres are represented by one centimetre.

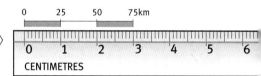

Scale One centimetre on the map represents **25** kilometres on the ground.

The distance between Bangor and Betws-y-Coed is about 25km

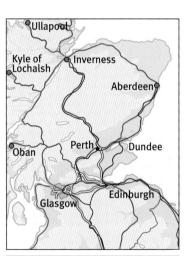

Scale One centimetre on the map represents **50** kilometres on the ground.

The distance between Perth and Edinburgh is about 50km

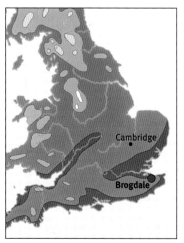

Scale One centimetre on the map represents **100** kilometres on the ground.

The distance between Cambridge and Brogdale is about 100km

Larger scale
smaller area
more detail

Smaller scale
larger area
less detail

On world maps the scale is only true along the equator.

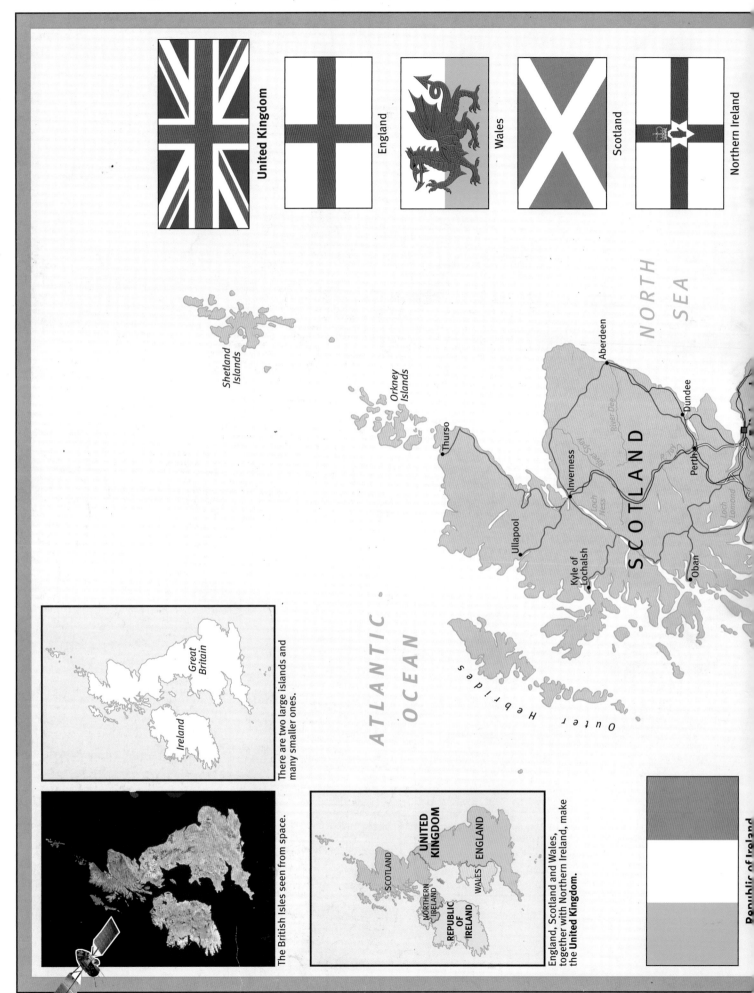

United Kingdom

England

Wales

Scotland

Northern Ireland

NORTH SEA

Shetland Islands

Orkney Islands

Thurso

Aberdeen

Dundee

Inverness

River Dee

Ullapool

Loch Ness

SCOTLAND

Perth

Loch Lomond

Kyle of Lochalsh

Oban

ATLANTIC OCEAN

Outer Hebrides

Great Britain

Ireland

There are two large islands and many smaller ones.

The British Isles seen from space.

UNITED KINGDOM

SCOTLAND

NORTHERN IRELAND

ENGLAND

WALES

REPUBLIC OF IRELAND

England, Scotland and Wales, together with Northern Ireland, make the **United Kingdom.**

Republic of Ireland

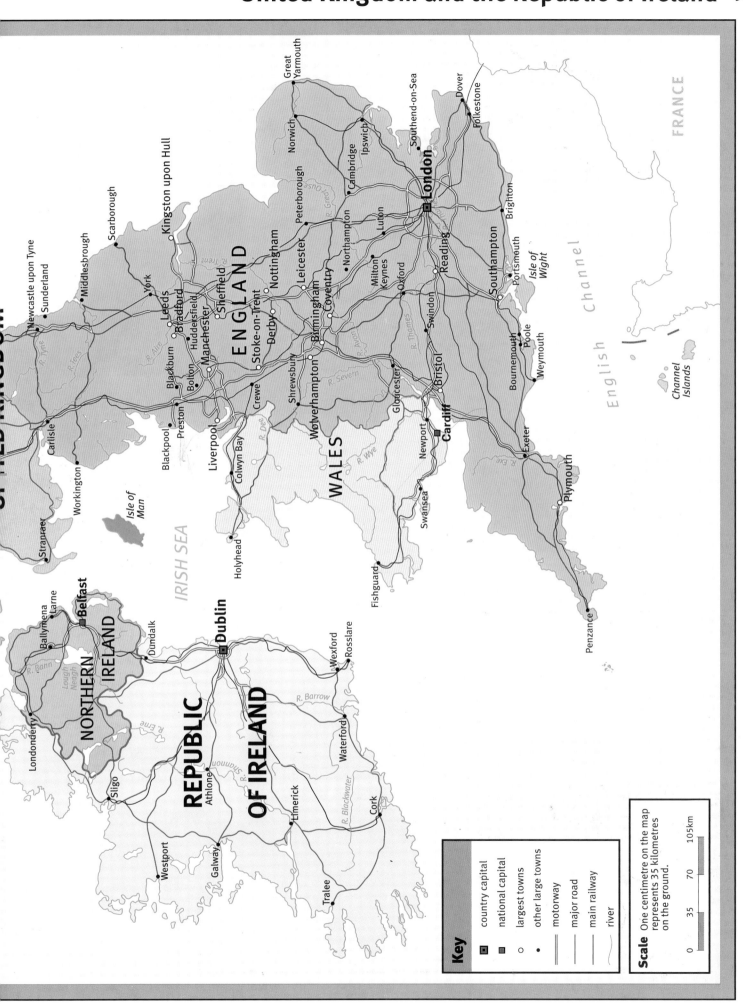

Key

country capital
national capital
largest towns
other large towns
motorway
major road
main railway
river

Scale One centimetre on the map represents 35 kilometres on the ground.

0   35   70   105km

FRANCE

English Channel

Channel Islands

IRISH SEA

Isle of Man

ENGLAND

WALES

NORTHERN IRELAND

REPUBLIC OF IRELAND

London
Dublin
Belfast
Cardiff

Great Yarmouth
Norwich
Ipswich
Cambridge
Southend-on-Sea
Dover
Folkestone
Peterborough
R. Great Ouse
Luton
Northampton
Brighton
Southampton
Portsmouth
Isle of Wight
Reading
Milton Keynes
Oxford
Swindon
R. Thames
Bournemouth
Poole
Weymouth
Exeter
R. Exe
Plymouth
Penzance

Kingston upon Hull
Scarborough
Newcastle upon Tyne
Sunderland
Middlesbrough
York
R. Tees
R. Tyne
Leeds
Bradford
Sheffield
Huddersfield
Nottingham
Leicester
Coventry
Birmingham
Derby
Stoke-on-Trent
Blackburn
Bolton
Manchester
R. Trent
R. Aire
Shrewsbury
Wolverhampton
R. Severn
Crewe
Gloucester
R. Avon
Bristol
Newport
Swansea
R. Wye
R. Dee
Colwyn Bay
Liverpool
Blackpool
Preston
Holyhead
Fishguard
Carlisle
Workington
Stranraer

Belfast
Ballymena
Larne
Londonderry
R. Bann
Lough Neagh
Dundalk
Sligo
Westport
Galway
Athlone
R. Shannon
R. Erne
Limerick
R. Barrow
Waterford
R. Blackwater
Cork
Tralee
Wexford
Rosslare

Oxford University Press

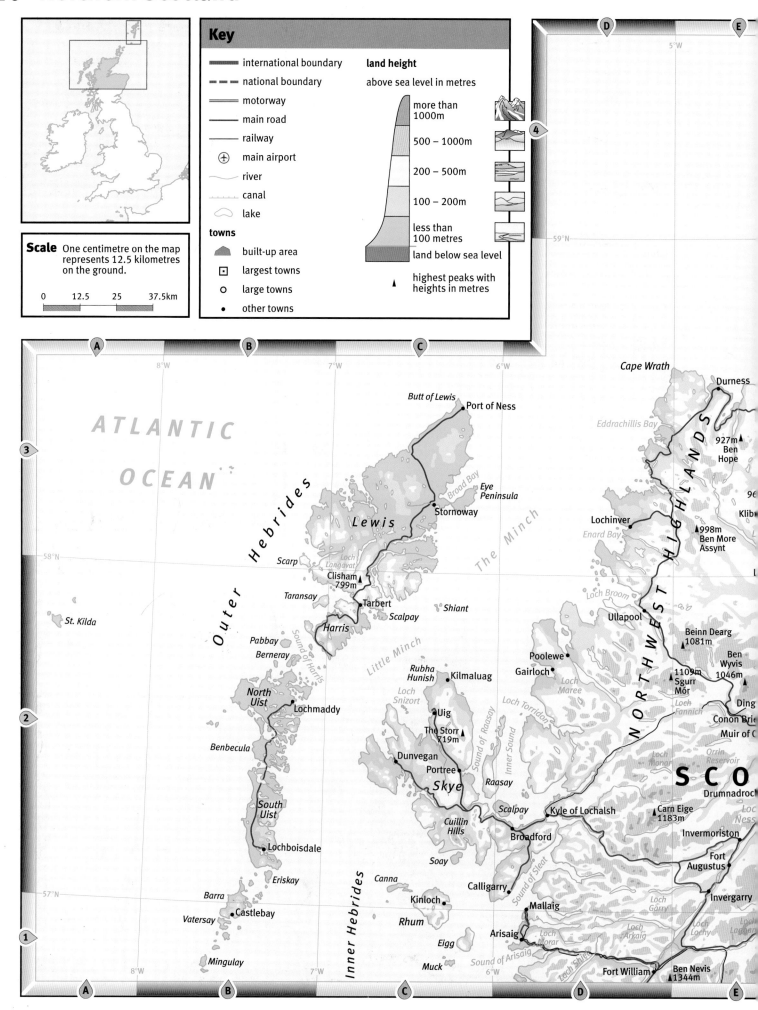

Key

▬▬▬	international boundary
▬ ▬ ▬	national boundary
══	motorway
────	main road
────	railway
⊕	main airport
～	river
┈┈┈	canal
⌒	lake

towns

⬙	built-up area
⊡	largest towns
○	large towns
•	other towns

land height

above sea level in metres

- more than 1000m
- 500 – 1000m
- 200 – 500m
- 100 – 200m
- less than 100 metres
- land below sea level

▲ highest peaks with heights in metres

Scale One centimetre on the map represents 12.5 kilometres on the ground.

0   12.5   25   37.5km

ATLANTIC OCEAN

Cape Wrath
Durness
Eddrachillis Bay
927m ▲ Ben Hope
Butt of Lewis
Port of Ness
Broad Bay
Eye Peninsula
Lochinver
Enard Bay
▲998m Ben More Assynt
Lewis
Stornoway
The Minch
Scarp
Loch Langavat
Clisham 799m ▲
Taransay
Tarbert
Scalpay
Shiant
Loch Broom
Ullapool
Beinn Dearg ▲1081m
Outer Hebrides
Harris
Little Minch
Pabbay
Berneray
Sound of Harris
Loch Maree
Poolewe
Gairloch
Ben Wyvis 1046m
St. Kilda
Rubha Hunish
Kilmaluag
1109m ▲ Sgurr Mór
Loch Snizort
Uig
Loch Torridon
Loch Fannich
North Uist
Lochmaddy
The Storr 719m ▲
Sound of Raasay
Inner Sound
Ding
Conon Brie
Muir of O
Benbecula
Dunvegan
Portree
Skye
Raasay
Loch Monar
Orrin Reservoir
SCO
Drumnadroc
South Uist
Cuillin Hills
Scalpay
Kyle of Lochalsh
Carn Eige ▲1183m
Loch Ness
Lochboisdale
Soay
Broadford
Invermoriston
Eriskay
Canna
Calligarry
Sound of Sleat
Fort Augustus
Invergarry
Barra
Kinloch
Mallaig
Loch Garry
Vatersay
Castlebay
Rhum
Arisaig
Loch Morar
Loch Arkaig
Loch Lochy
Mingulay
Eigg
Muck
Sound of Arisaig
Fort William
Ben Nevis ▲1344m
Inner Hebrides

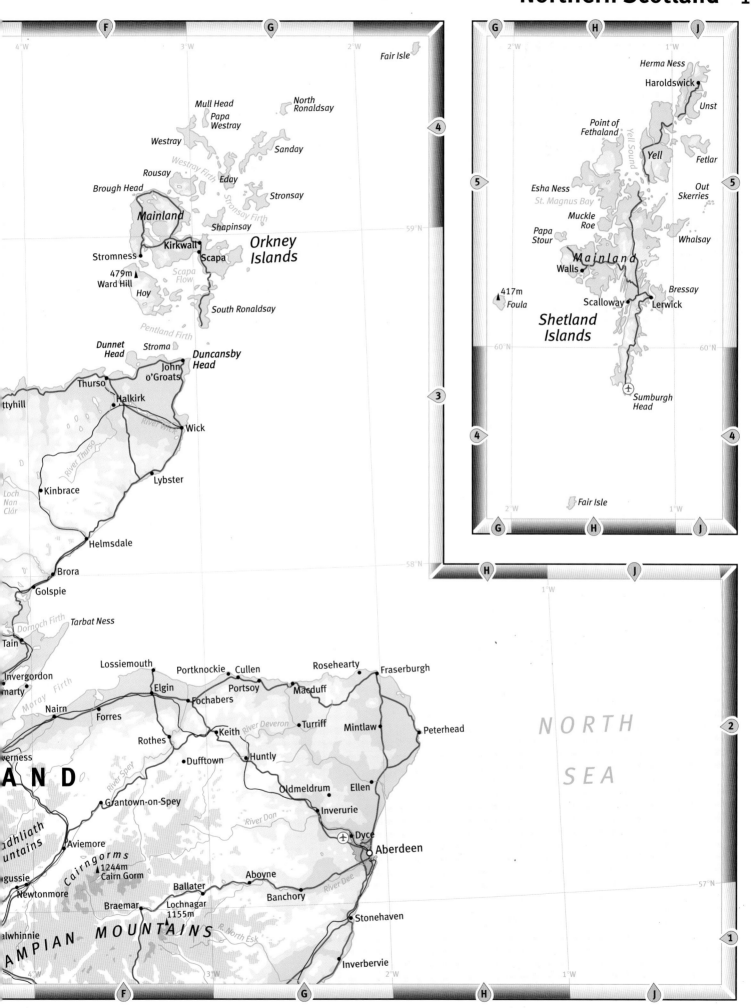

Orkney Islands

Fair Isle
Mull Head
Papa Westray
North Ronaldsay
Westray
Sanday
Rousay
Eday
Brough Head
Stronsay
Mainland
Shapinsay
Stromness
Kirkwall
Scapa
479m Ward Hill
Hoy
Scapa Flow
South Ronaldsay
Pentland Firth
Westray Firth
Stronsay Firth

Shetland Islands

Herma Ness
Haroldswick
Unst
Point of Fethaland
Yell
Fetlar
Esha Ness
Out Skerries
St. Magnus Bay
Muckle Roe
Whalsay
Papa Stour
Mainland
Walls
Bressay
417m Foula
Scalloway
Lerwick
Sumburgh Head
Yell Sound
Fair Isle

Dunnet Head
Stroma
Duncansby Head
Thurso
John o'Groats
Halkirk
Wick
ttyhill
Lybster
Kinbrace
Loch Nan Clàr
Helmsdale
Brora
Golspie
Dornoch Firth
Tarbat Ness
Tain
Invergordon
marty
Lossiemouth
Portknockie
Cullen
Rosehearty
Fraserburgh
Elgin
Portsoy
Macduff
Nairn
Fochabers
Forres
Turriff
Mintlaw
Peterhead
Rothes
Keith
River Deveron
Dufftown
Huntly
verness
Oldmeldrum
Ellen
Grantown-on-Spey
Inverurie
River Don
Aviemore
Dyce
adhliath untains
Cairngorms
Aberdeen
gussie
1244m Cairn Gorm
Aboyne
Newtonmore
Ballater
Banchory
River Dee
Braemar
Lochnagar 1155m
Stonehaven
alwhinnie
AMPIAN MOUNTAINS
R. North Esk
Inverbervie
Moray Firth
River Spey
AND
River Thurso
River Wick

NORTH
SEA

Scale One centimetre on the map represents 12.5 kilometres on the ground.

0   12.5   25   37.5km

SCOTLAND

NORTHERN IRELAND

GRAMPIAN MOUNTAINS

Ben Nevis 1344m
Blackwater Reservoir
Kinlochleven
Fort William
Loch Shiel
Tobermory
Lochaline
Sound of Mull
Craignure
Lismore
Ben Lawers 1214m
Loch Lyon
Loch Etive
Tyndrum
Muck
Coll
Tiree
Ulva
967m Ben More
Mull
Kerrera
Oban
1124m Ben Cruachan
River Orchy
Crianlarich
Ben More 1174m
Loche
Iona
Fionnphort
Ross of Mull
Firth of Lorn
Inveraray
974m Ben Lomond
Ca
Scarba
Furnace
Strachur
Loch
Colonsay
Scalasaig
Lochgilphead
Garelochhead
Loch Long
Campsie
Oronsay
Loch Lomond
Helensburgh
Jura
Sound of Jura
Dunoon
Greenock
Dumbarton
Kirkint
Port Askaig
Craighouse
Tarbert
Rothesay
Port Glasgow
Clydebank
Bearsden
Co
Kennacraig
Bute
Largs
Johnstone
Paisley
Gl
Islay
Gigha
Clachan
Newton Mearns
Ea Ki
Barrhead
Han
Portnahaven
Kintyre
Lochranza
Goat Fell 874m
Ardrossan
Irvine
Stewarton
Darvel
Saltcoats
Kilmarnock
Mull of Oa
Port Ellen
Brodick
Arran
River Ay
Firth of Clyde
Prestwick
Campbeltown
Southend
Mull of Kintyre
Ailsa Craig
Ayr
Cun
Maybole
New Cumnock
River Doon
Malin Head
Giant's Causeway
Rathlin Island
Fair Head
North Channel
Girvan
SOUTHE
Inishowen Peninsula
615m Slieve Snaght
Portrush
Bushmills
Ballycastle
Rathlin Sound
Ballantrae
Ne Gallowa
Creeslough
Buncrana
Coleraine
R. Bush
Antrim Mountains
Corsewall Point
Lough Foyle
Ballymoney
Cairnryan
Newton Stewart
Gatehou of Fl
Kilmacrenan
Limavady
Carnlough
Stranraer
Wigtown
Letterkenny
Londonderry
Dungiven
River Main
River Bann
Glenluce
Kirkcud
Lough Swilly
Ballybofey
Lifford
Strabane
Sperrin Mountains
683m Sawel
Maghera
Ballymena
Island Magee
Whithorn
R. Finn
Newtownstewart
Magherafelt
Larne
R. Derg
Randalstown
Carrickfergus
Drummore
Donegal
NORTHERN IRELAND
Omagh
Cookstown
Antrim
Newtownabbey
Belfast Lough
Bangor
Donaghadee
Mull of Galloway
Lough Derg
Coalisland
Lough Neagh
Crumlin
Belfast
Newtownards
Irvinestown
Dungannon
Lisburn
Ards Peninsula
Point of
Lower Lough Erne
Aughnacloy
Portadown
Lurgan
Craigavon
Dromore
Saintfield
R. Blackwater
Armagh
R. Lagan
Ramsey
Manorhamilton
Enniskillen
Banbridge
Strangford Lough
Downpatrick
Kirk Michael
Snaefell 620m
Keady
River Bann
Peel
R. Shannon
Upper Lough Erne
Lisnaskea
Monaghan
Newtownhamilton
Newcastle
St. John's Point
Isle Man
Clones
Newry
852m Slieve Donard
Douglas
Castleblayney
Warrenpoint
Mourne Mtns.
Port Erin
Crossmaglen
Kilkeel
Calf of Man
Castletown

Key

—————— international boundary
- - - - - national boundary
═══════ motorway
————— main road
————— railway
⊕ main airport
river
canal
⌒ lake

towns

⬟ built-up area
⊡ largest towns
○ large towns
• other towns

land height

above sea level in metres

more than 1000m
500 – 1000m
200 – 500m
100 – 200m
less than 100 metres
land below sea level

▲ highest peaks with heights in metres

Pitlochry
erfeldy
River Tay
Kirriemuir
Blairgowrie
Brechin
Montrose
Milton Ness
R. South Esk
Forfar
Arbroath
Sidlaw Hills
Carnoustie
Dundee
Firth of Tay
jeff
Perth
Auchterarder
Leuchars
St. Andrews
Cupar
Auchtermuchty
Anstruther
River Earn
ne
Ochil Hills
Loch Leven
Glenrothes
Kinross
Buckhaven
Tillicoultry
Cowdenbeath
Kirkcaldy
Alloa
Dunfermline
Grangemouth
Inverkeithing
lkirk
ernauld
Linlithgow
Edinburgh
North Berwick
Dunbar
athgate
Livingston
Musselburgh
Haddington
St. Abb's Head
well
Dalkeith
Lammermuir Hills
Eyemouth
haw
Penicuik
Duns
Berwick-upon-Tweed
Pentland Hills
Holy Island
Lanark
Peebles
Galashiels
Coldstream
Bamburgh
Biggar
Melrose
River Tweed
Kelso
PLANDS
Broad Law ▲840m
Selkirk
Wooler
The Cheviot 815m
Alnwick
River Tweed
Hawick
Jedburgh
R. Teviot
R. Aln
uhar
Moffat
Peel Fell 602m
Cheviot Hills
Amble
Daer Reservoir
Ettrick Water
River Coquet
hill
Langholm
Lockerbie
Kielder Water
R. North Tyne
R. Wansbeck
Ashington
Dumfries
Blyth
Cramlington
Whitley Bay
Newcastle upon Tyne
Tynemouth
South Shields
Annan
R. Irthing
Gateshead
las
Brampton
Haltwhistle
Hexham
R. Tyne
Sunderland
Dalbeattie
Carlisle
Consett
Washington
Houghton-le-Spring
Solway Firth
Wigton
Chester-le-Street
River Eden
Cross Fell 893m▲
PENNINES
Durham
Peterlee
Maryport
River Wear
Spennymoor
Hartlepool
Workington
Skiddaw 931m▲
Penrith
Mickle Fell▲ 790m
Bishop Auckland
Billingham
Redcar
Cockermouth
Derwent
River Tees
Newton Aycliffe
Stockton-on-Tees
Middlesbrough
Whitehaven
Derwent Water
Keswick
Ullswater
Appleby-in-Westmorland
Barnard Castle
Darlington
Thornaby-on-Tees
Guisborough
Whitby
Bees Head
Helvellyn ▲950m
Brough
R. Tees
Scafell Pike 978m▲
Lake District
ENGLAND
Cleveland Hills
North York Moors
River Esk
Seascale
West Water
Windermere
Windermere
Ambleside
Richmond
Northallerton
Scarborough
Coniston Water
Kendal
River Swale
Thirsk
Pickering
Vale of Pickering
Filey
Whernside 737m▲
River Ure
Leyburn
River Wharfe
Great Whernside 704m
Vale of York
Malton
Ulverston
Ingleborough▲ 723m
693m▲ Pen-y-Ghent
Ripon
Yorkshire Wolds
Bridlington
Barrow-in-Furness
Carnforth
Settle
River Nidd
Haxby
Great Driffield
Morecambe
Lancaster
Ward's Stone 560m▲
River Aire
Knaresborough
Heysham
Harrogate
York

NORTH SEA

IRISH SEA

Isle of Man
Port Erin
Calf of Man
Castletown

Barrow-in-Furness
Carnforth
Morecambe
Lancaster
Heysham

Warrenpoint
Kilkeel

Fleetwood
Thornton
Blackpool
Lytham St. Anne's
Preston
Bla

Balbriggan

Southport
Leyland
Da

Formby
Skelmersdale
Kirkby
Wig

Swords
Bootle
Wallasey
St. Helen
Liverpool

Dublin
Birkenhead
Widnes
Wa

Dún Laoghaire
Carmel Head
Amlwch
Anglesey
Llandudno
Prestatyn
Holywell
River Dee
Ellesmere Port
Runco

Bray
Holyhead
Llangefni
Menai Bridge
Conwy
Colwyn Bay
Rhyl
Holywell
Flint
Connah's Quay
Chester
Winsf

Holy Island
Bangor
Denbigh
Mold
Lake Brenig
Ruthin

Bethesda
Caernarfon
Llanrwst
Betws-y-Coed
Lake Chwyd
Wrexham
Nantw

Caernarfon Bay
Snowdon 1085m

Wicklow

Lleyn Peninsula
Porthmadog
Blaenau Ffestiniog
Corwen
Llangollen
Ruabon
Wh

Bardsey Island
Pwllheli
Harlech
Bala
Bala Lake
Oswestry
Chirk
Dr

Arklow

Dolgellau
Lake Vyrnwy
R. Vyrnwy
Shrewsbury
Wel

Barmouth
892m Cadair Idris
CAMBRIAN MOUNTAINS
R. Dyfi
Welshpool

Cahore Point

Tywyn
Machynlleth
Montgomery
The W

Cardigan Bay
Plynlimon 752m
Newtown
Wenlock Edge

Aberystwyth
Llanidloes
Ludl

WALES

Rhayader
Knighton
River

Aberaeron
New Quay
Claerwen Reservoir
Llandrindod Wells
Kington
Leomi

Cemaes Head
Lake Brianne Reservoir
Builth Wells

St. George's Channel
Strumble Head
Newport
Cardigan
River Teifi
Lampeter
Mynydd Eppynt
Hay-on-Wye
Heref

Newcastle Emlyn
Llandovery
Black Mountains

St. David's Head
Fishguard
Preseli Mountains
River Usk
Brecon
Ross-on-Wye

St. Brides Bay
Carmarthen
St. Clears
Llandeilo
Brecon Beacons
886m
Abergavenny
Monmouth
Cin

Cross Hands
Ammanford
Tredegar
Ebbw Vale

Milford Haven
Kidwelly
Merthyr Tydfil
Abertillery

Saundersfoot
Llanelli
Pontardulais
Aberdare
Mountain Ash
Pontypool
Cwmbran
R. Wye

Pembroke Dock
Tenby
Burry Port
Neath
Rhondda
Gelligaer
Chepstow

Pembroke
Gorseinon
Maesteg
Pontypridd
Caerphilly
Newport

Carmarthen Bay
Swansea
Port Talbot
Mangotsf

Worms Head
Gower
Porthcawl
Bridgend
Cardiff
Clevedon
Bristol
Kings

Bristol Channel
Barry
Penarth
Weston-super-Mare
Keyn

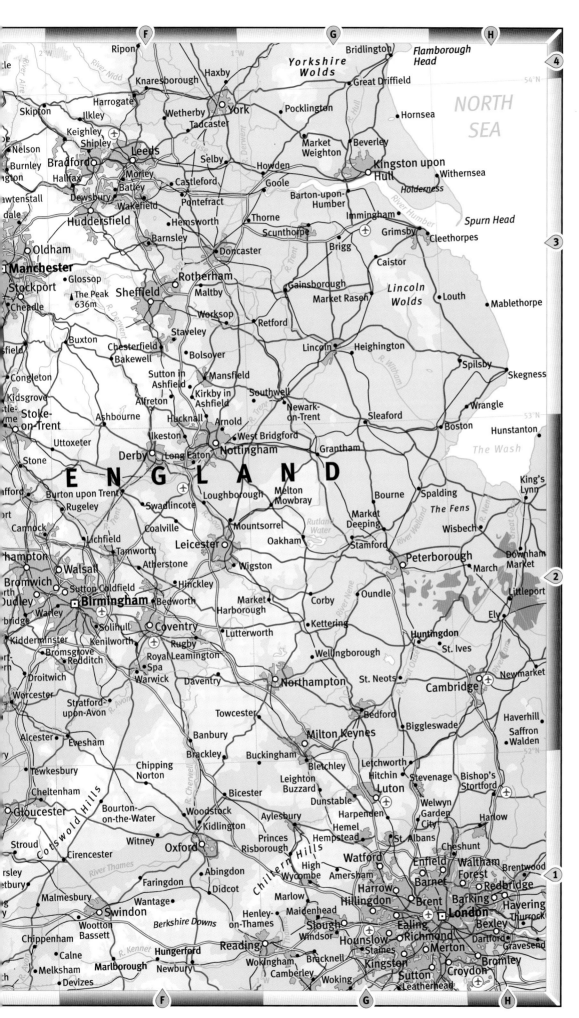

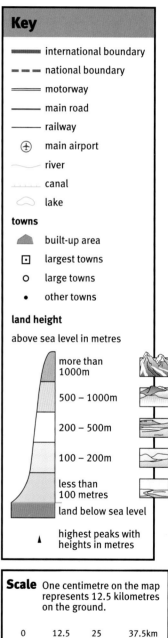

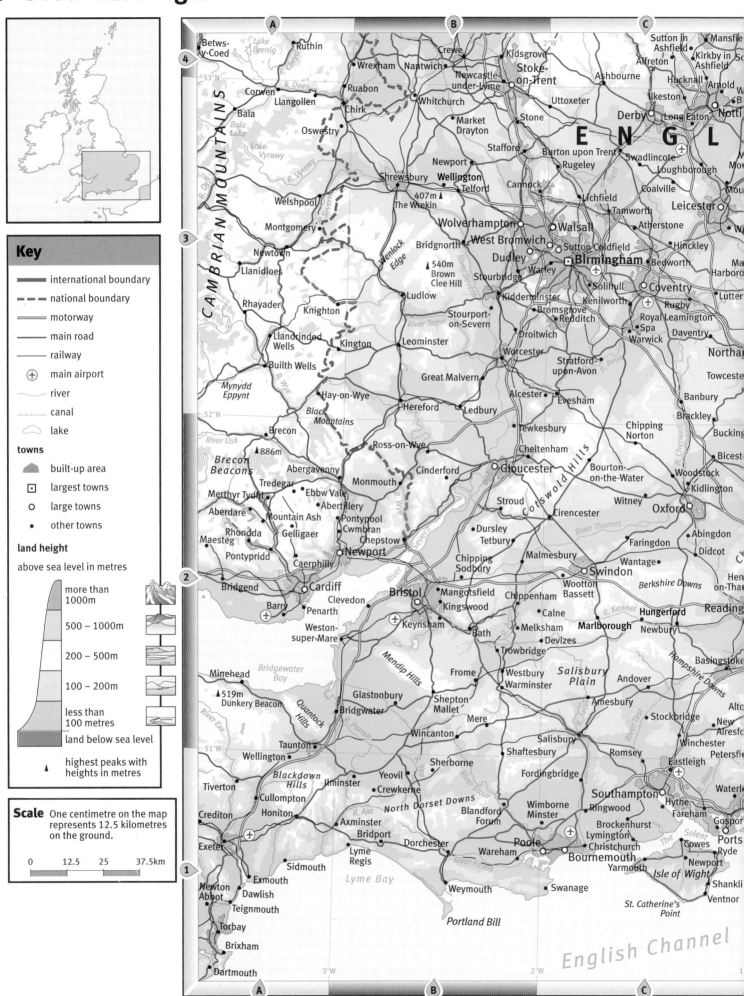

Key

	international boundary
	national boundary
	motorway
	main road
	railway
⊕	main airport
	river
	canal
	lake

towns

	built-up area
⊡	largest towns
○	large towns
•	other towns

land height

above sea level in metres

more than 1000m

500 – 1000m

200 – 500m

100 – 200m

less than 100 metres

land below sea level

▲ highest peaks with heights in metres

Scale One centimetre on the map represents 12.5 kilometres on the ground.

0   12.5   25   37.5km

CAMBRIAN MOUNTAINS

Betws-y-Coed · Ruthin · Wrexham · Nantwich · Crewe · Kidsgrove · Stoke-on-Trent · Sutton in Ashfield · Mansfie · Kirkby in · Alfreton · Hucknall · Arnold · Nott

Lake Brenig · Corwen · Ruabon · Whitchurch · Newcastle-under-Lyme · Ashbourne · Ilkeston · Long Eaton

Llangollen · Chirk · Stone · Uttoxeter · Derby

Bala · Oswestry · Market Drayton · Stafford · Burton upon Trent · Swadlincote

Bala Lake · Stafford · Cannock · Rugeley · Loughborough · Coalville

R. Dee · Welshpool · Shrewsbury · Wellington · Telford · Lichfield · Tamworth · Leicester

Lake Vyrnwy · The Wrekin 407m▲ · Wolverhampton · Walsall · Atherstone

Montgomery · Bridgnorth · West Bromwich · Sutton Coldfield · Hinckley

Newtown · Brown Clee Hill 540m▲ · Dudley · Birmingham · Bedworth · Harbor

Llanidloes · Wenlock Edge · Stourbridge · Warley · Solihull · Coventry · Lutter

Rhayader · Ludlow · Kidderminster · Kenilworth · Rugby

Knighton · Stourport-on-Severn · Bromsgrove · Redditch · Royal Leamington Spa · Daventry · Northa

Llandrindod Wells · Kington · Leominster · Droitwich · Warwick

Builth Wells · River Teme · Worcester · Stratford-upon-Avon

Mynydd Eppynt · Hay-on-Wye · Great Malvern · Alcester · Evesham · Towceste

Black Mountains · Hereford · Ledbury · Banbury

Brecon · Ross-on-Wye · Tewkesbury · Chipping Norton · Brackley · Bucking

886m▲ · Cinderford · Cheltenham · Cotswold Hills · Bicest

Brecon Beacons · Abergavenny · Monmouth · Gloucester · Bourton-on-the-Water · Woodstock · Kidlington

Tredegar · Stroud · Cirencester · Witney · Oxford

Merthyr Tydfil · Ebbw Vale · Abertillery · Pontypool · Cwmbran · Dursley · Malmesbury · Abingdon · Didcot

Aberdare · Mountain Ash · Gelligaer · Chepstow · Tetbury · Faringdon · Wantage · Hen-on-Tha

Rhondda · Newport · Chipping Sodbury · Swindon · Berkshire Downs

Maesteg · Pontypridd · Caerphilly · Wootton Bassett · Reading

Bridgend · Cardiff · Clevedon · Bristol · Mangotsfield · Chippenham · Calne · Hungerford

Barry · Penarth · Kingswood · River Kennet · Marlborough · Newbury

Weston-super-Mare · Keynsham · Melksham · Devizes

Bath · Trowbridge · Basingstoke

Minehead · Bridgewater Bay · Mendip Hills · Frome · Westbury · Warminster · Salisbury Plain · Andover · Hampshire Downs

519m▲ Dunkery Beacon · Glastonbury · Shepton Mallet · Amesbury · Stockbridge · New Alresfo

River Exe · Quantock Hills · Bridgwater · Mere · Salisbury · Winchester · Petersfie

Taunton · Wincanton · Shaftesbury · Romsey · Eastleigh

Wellington · Blackdown Hills · Ilminster · Yeovil · Sherborne · Fordingbridge · Southampton

Tiverton · Crewkerne · North Dorset Downs · Wimborne Minster · Ringwood · Hythe · Fareham

Cullompton · Honiton · Blandford Forum · Brockenhurst · Lymington · Gospo

Crediton · Axminster · Bridport · Dorchester · Poole · Christchurch · Cowes · Ports

Exeter · Lyme Regis · Wareham · Bournemouth · Ryde

Newton Abbot · Dawlish · Sidmouth · Lyme Bay · Weymouth · Swanage · Newport · Yarmouth · Isle of Wight · Shankli

Teignmouth · Portland Bill · St. Catherine's Point · Ventnor

Torbay

Brixham

Dartmouth · English Channel

Skegness
Wrangle
Sleaford
Boston
Hunstanton
Wells-next-the-Sea
Cromer
Grantham
The Wash
Fakenham
North Walsham
Bourne
Spalding
Aylsham
River Bure
Market Deeping
King's Lynn
The Fens
Rutland Water
Stamford
Wisbech
Swaffham
East Dereham
Norwich
Acle
Great Yarmouth
Peterborough
Downham Market
Attleborough
Wymondham
March
NORTH SEA
Corby
Oundle
Littleport
Thetford
Diss
Bungay
Beccles
Lowestoft
Kettering
Ely
Mildenhall
River Waveney
Southwold
Huntingdon
St. Ives
Wellingborough
Newmarket
Bury St. Edmunds
Stowmarket
Saxmundham
Wickham Market
St. Neots
Cambridge
Aldeburgh
Bedford
Haverhill
Woodbridge
Biggleswade
Saffron Walden
Sudbury
Ipswich
ilton Keynes
Letchworth
River Stour
Felixstowe
etchley
Hitchin
Stevenage
Bishop's Stortford
Braintree
Harwich
Leighton Buzzard
Luton
Welwyn Garden City
Harlow
River Colne
Colchester
Walton-on-the-Naze
unstable
Harpenden
Hemel Hempstead
St. Albans
Chelmsford
Witham
Clacton-on-Sea
ough
Watford
Cheshunt
Southminster
s
Amersham
Enfield
Waltham Forest
Brentwood
Rayleigh
Harrow
Barnet
Redbridge
Basildon
Hillingdon
Brent
Barking
Havering
Southend-on-Sea
head
London
Ealing
Bexley
Thurrock
Sheerness
Hounslow
Richmond
Dartford
Gravesend
Herne Bay
Margate
North Foreland
nell
Staines
Merton
Chatham
Whitstable
Ramsgate
gham
Kingston
Bromley
Gillingham
Sittingbourne
Canterbury
mberley
Sutton
Croydon
Deal
Woking
Leatherhead
Sevenoaks
Maidstone
North Downs
arnborough
Reigate
Tonbridge
Ashford
Dover
ershot
Guildford
Redhill
Dorking
Strait of Dover
ham
Godalming
North Downs
East Grinstead
Royal Tunbridge Wells
Folkestone
Nieuwpoort
aslemere
R. Arun
Crawley
Hythe
Veurne
dhurst
Horsham
Crowborough
New Romney
BELGIUM
Billingshurst
Uckfield
Rye
Dungeness
Dunkerque
Downs
Haywards Heath
Calais
ittlehampton
Lewes
Hailsham
Ardres
Cassel
ester
Hove
Brighton
Hastings
Bexhill
St-Omer
Bognor Regis
Worthing
Seaford
Eastbourne
Boulogne-sur-Mer
Hazebrouck
y Bill
Beachy Head
Lillers
Le Touquet-Paris-Plage
FRANCE
Béthune

53°N
52°N
51°N
0°   1°E   2°E

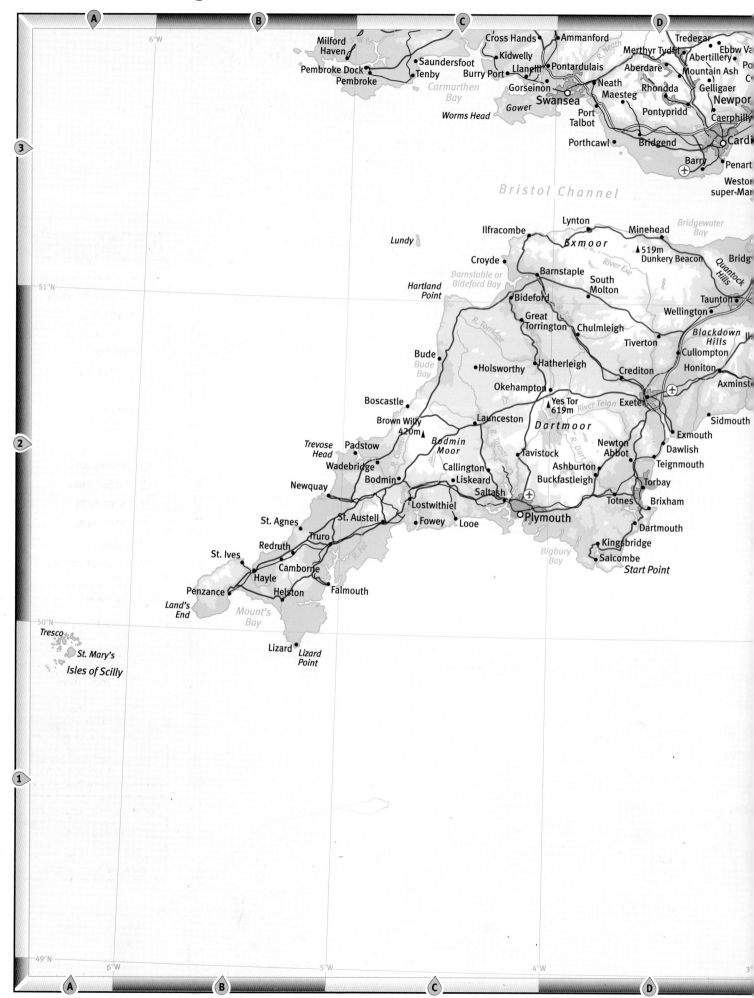

Carmarthen Bay

Milford Haven
Pembroke Dock
Pembroke
Saundersfoot
Tenby
Cross Hands
Ammanford
Kidwelly
Burry Port
Llanelli
Pontardulais
Gorseinon
Gower
Worms Head
Swansea
Neath
Maesteg
Port Talbot
Porthcawl
Bridgend
Tredegar
Merthyr Tydfil
Abertillery
Ebbw Va
Aberdare
Mountain Ash
Rhondda
Gelligaer
Pontypridd
Caerphilly
Newpor
Cardi
Barry
Penart
Westor
super-Mar

Bristol Channel

Lundy
Ilfracombe
Croyde
Barnstable or Bideford Bay
Hartland Point
Lynton
Minehead
Bridgewater Bay
Exmoor
▲519m
Dunkery Beacon
River Exe
Quantock Hills
Bridg
Barnstaple
South Molton
Bideford
Great Torrington
Chulmleigh
Tiverton
Blackdown Hills
Cullompton
Honiton
Taunton
Wellington
Axminst
Bude
Bude Bay
Holsworthy
Hatherleigh
Okehampton
Crediton
Exeter
Sidmouth
Boscastle
Brown Willy 420m▲
Launceston
Yes Tor 619m▲
Dartmoor
River Teign
Exmouth
Trevose Head
Padstow
Bodmin Moor
R. Camel
Tavistock
R. Tamar
R. Dart
Newton Abbot
Dawlish
Wadebridge
Bodmin
Callington
Liskeard
Ashburton
Buckfastleigh
Teignmouth
Newquay
Saltash
Plymouth
Totnes
Torbay
Brixham
St. Agnes
St. Austell
Lostwithiel
Fowey
Looe
Dartmouth
Redruth
Truro
R. Fal
Kingsbridge
Bigbury Bay
Salcombe
Start Point
St. Ives
Camborne
Hayle
Penzance
Land's End
Helston
Falmouth
Mount's Bay
Tresco
St. Mary's
Isles of Scilly
Lizard
Lizard Point

6°W 5°W 4°W
51°N
50°N
49°N
A B C D
1 2 3

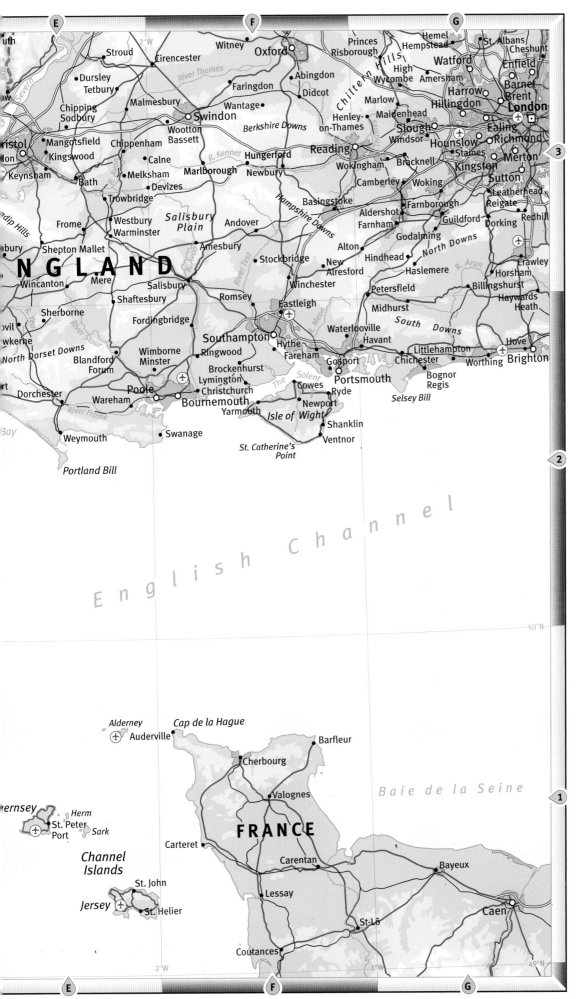

Key

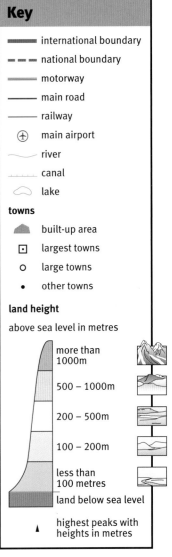

- ▬▬▬ international boundary
- ▬ ▬ ▬ national boundary
- ▬▬ motorway
- ▬▬ main road
- ▬ railway
- ✈ main airport
- ∿ river
- ⊥⊥⊥ canal
- ⌒ lake

towns
- 🔺 built-up area
- ☐ largest towns
- ○ large towns
- • other towns

land height
above sea level in metres
- more than 1000m
- 500 – 1000m
- 200 – 500m
- 100 – 200m
- less than 100 metres
- land below sea level
- ▲ highest peaks with heights in metres

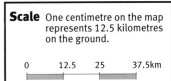

Scale One centimetre on the map represents 12.5 kilometres on the ground.

0   12.5   25   37.5km

Highest mountains

few places in Britain are more than 1000 metres high

Mountains

steep rocky places

Moors and uplands

high windswept places with heather and rough grass

Hills

smooth slopes and gentle valleys

Low land

flat marshy land with wide rivers

Key

colours show land height above sea level in metres

- more than 1000m
- 500 – 1000m
- 200 – 500m
- 100 – 200m
- less than 100 metres
- land below sea level

▲ highest peaks with heights in metres

〜 river

lake

Scale One centimetre on the map represents 45 kilometres on the ground.

0   45   90   135km

Shetland Islands

Orkney Islands

Cape Wrath

Outer Hebrides

Lewis

Skye

NORTHWEST HIGHLANDS

Great Glen

Loch Ness

River Spey

Cairngorms

River Dee

1344m ▲ Ben Nevis

GRAMPIAN MOUNTAINS

R. Tay

Mull

Loch Lomond

Firth of Forth

R. Clyde

Islay

NORTH SEA

SOUTHERN UPLANDS

River Tweed

Cheviot Hills

R. Tyne

North Channel

Antrim Mountains

R. Bann

Loch Neagh

River Erne

Firth of Clyde

Isle of Man

Lake District

978m ▲ Scafell Pike

River Eden

River Tees

P E N N I N E S

North York Moors

River Ouse

▲ 852m Slieve Donard

IRISH SEA

River Aire

River Humber

Ireland

Loch Corrib

River Boyne

River Shannon

River Liffey

Wicklow Mountains

R. Barrow

Anglesey

1085m ▲ Snowdon

CAMBRIAN MOUNTAINS

R. Mersey

Great Britain

R. Trent

The Wash

R. Wensum

The Fens

River Suir

Cardigan Bay

River Teifi

River Wye

River Avon

River Great Ouse

River Stour

River Blackwater

River Usk

River Severn

Cotswold Hills

Chiltern Hills

▲ 1041m Carrantuohill

R. Tywi

Brecon Beacons

River Thames

St. George's Channel

Salisbury Plain

North Downs

Bristol Channel

Exmoor

South Downs

R. Exe

Isle of Wight

Strait of Dover

ATLANTIC OCEAN

Dartmoor

English Channel

Land's End

Isles of Scilly

Channel Islands

Oxford University Press
ansverse Mercator Projection

Winter

| Jan. | Feb. | Mar. | Apr. | May | June | July | Aug. | Sep. | Oct. | Nov. | Dec. |

average temperature

Summer

| Jan. | Feb. | Mar. | Apr. | May | June | July | Aug. | Sep. | Oct. | Nov. | Dec. |

average temperature

January temperature

Key

average temperature

	over 6°C	**cool**
	4–6°C	
	2–4°C	**cold**
	0–2°C	
	below 0°C	**very cold**

○ the coldest place in Britain

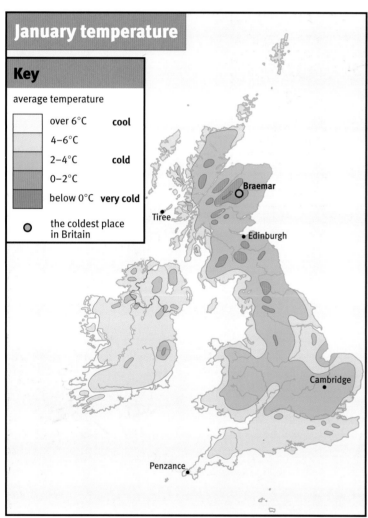

Braemar
Tiree
Edinburgh
Cambridge
Penzance

July temperature

Key

average temperature

	over 16°C	**hot**
	14–16°C	
	12–14°C	**warm**
	10–12°C	
	below 10°C	**mild**

● the hottest place in Britain

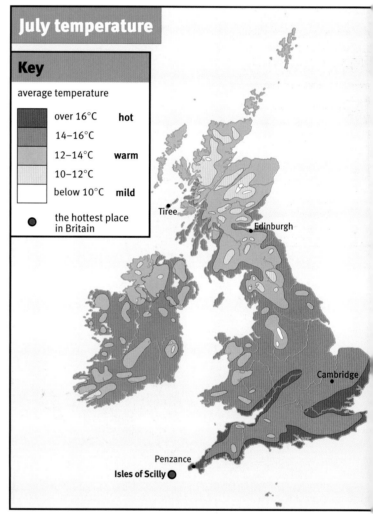

Tiree
Edinburgh
Cambridge
Penzance
Isles of Scilly ○

Climate regions

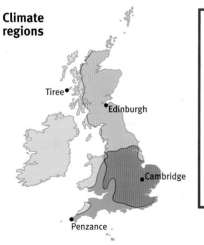

Tiree
Edinburgh
Cambridge
Penzance

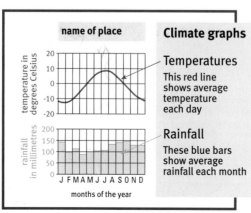

name of place

Climate graphs

Temperatures
This red line shows average temperature each day

Rainfall
These blue bars show average rainfall each month

temperature in degrees Celsius

rainfall in millimetres

months of the year

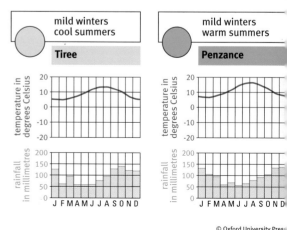

mild winters cool summers

Tiree

mild winters warm summers

Penzance

temperature in degrees Celsius

rainfall in millimetres

J F M A M J J A S O N D

© Oxford University Press
Transverse Mercator Projection

average rainfall

2400mm	very wet
2200mm	quite wet
2000mm	
1800mm	
1600mm	wet
1400mm	
1200mm	
1000mm	quite dry
800mm	
600mm	very dry
400mm	
200mm	

Wet winds from the west rise and cool to give rain and snow. Mountains are the wettest places in the British Isles.

West is wetter

East is drier

| Jan. | Feb. | Mar. | Apr. | May | June | July | Aug. | Sep. | Oct. | Nov. | Dec. |

Annual rainfall

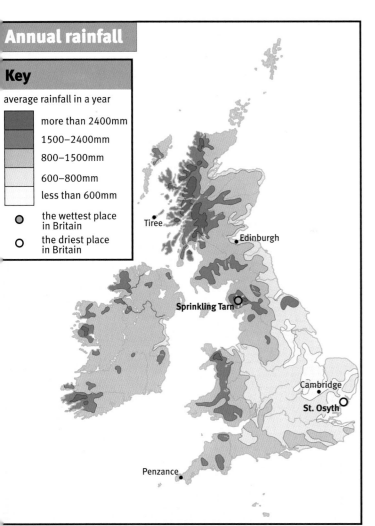

Key

average rainfall in a year

- more than 2400mm
- 1500–2400mm
- 800–1500mm
- 600–800mm
- less than 600mm
- ● the wettest place in Britain
- ○ the driest place in Britain

Tiree

Edinburgh

Sprinkling Tarn

Cambridge

St. Osyth

Penzance

Water supply

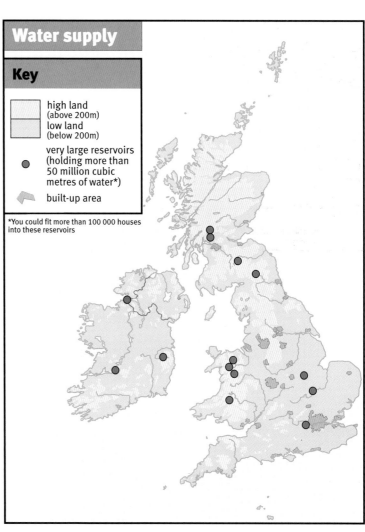

Key

- high land (above 200m)
- low land (below 200m)
- ● very large reservoirs (holding more than 50 million cubic metres of water*)
- built-up area

*You could fit more than 100 000 houses into these reservoirs

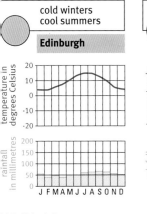

cold winters cool summers

Edinburgh

temperature in degrees Celsius

20
10
0
-10
-20

rainfall in millimetres

200
150
100
50

J F M A M J J A S O N D

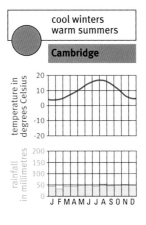

cool winters warm summers

Cambridge

temperature in degrees Celsius

20
10
0
-10
-20

rainfall in millimetres

200
150
100
50

J F M A M J J A S O N D

The water cycle

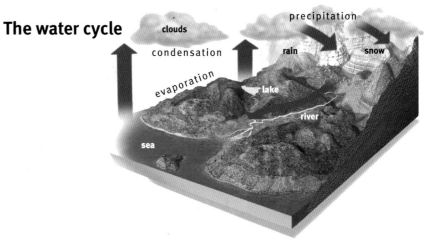

precipitation

clouds

condensation

rain

snow

evaporation

lake

river

sea

Cities and towns
People live in settlements of different sizes

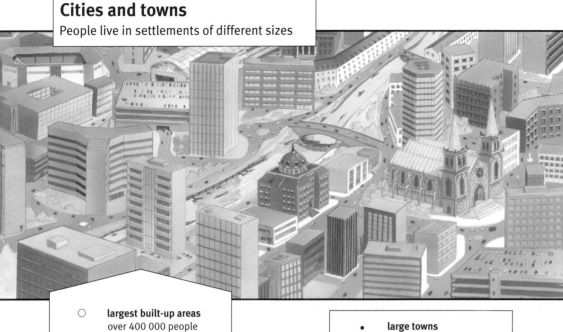

○ **largest built-up areas**
over 400 000 people

◉ **largest towns**
100 000 – 400 000 people

• **large towns**
25 000 – 100 000

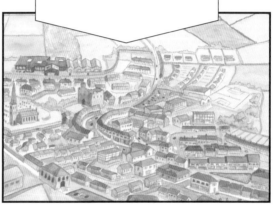

small towns and villages
under 25 000 people
(not shown on the map)

Population density
The number of people that live in an area

very crowded
over 250 people living
in a square kilometre

quite crowded
50 – 250 people living
in a square kilometre

quite empty
under 50 people living
in a square kilometre

Where people live
If there were 100 people in the
United Kingdom, this is where
they would live:

England
Scotland
Wales
Northern
Ireland

Population pyramid
If there were 100 people in the United Kingdom,
this is how old they would be:

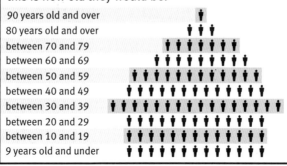

90 years old and over
80 years old and over
between 70 and 79
between 60 and 69
between 50 and 59
between 40 and 49
between 30 and 39
between 20 and 29
between 10 and 19
9 years old and under

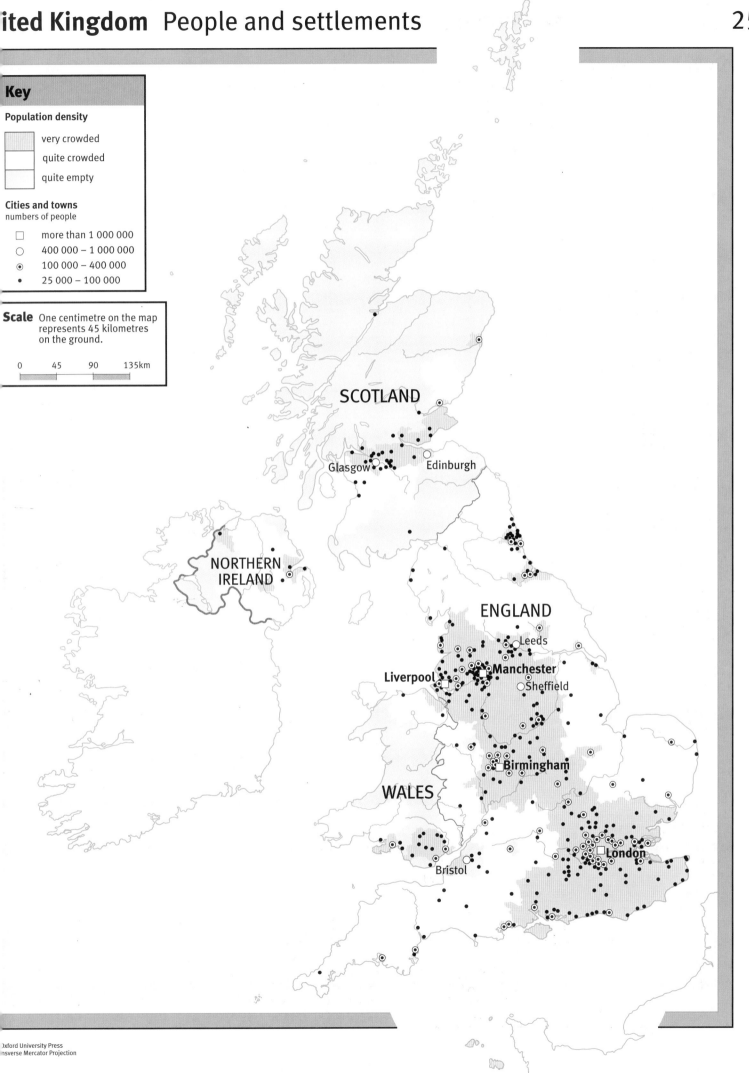

Key

Population density

- very crowded
- quite crowded
- quite empty

Cities and towns
numbers of people

- ☐ more than 1 000 000
- ○ 400 000 – 1 000 000
- ◉ 100 000 – 400 000
- • 25 000 – 100 000

Scale One centimetre on the map represents 45 kilometres on the ground.

0   45   90   135km

SCOTLAND

Glasgow   Edinburgh

NORTHERN
IRELAND

ENGLAND

Leeds

Liverpool   Manchester
Sheffield

Birmingham

WALES

London

Bristol

Oxford University Press
Transverse Mercator Projection

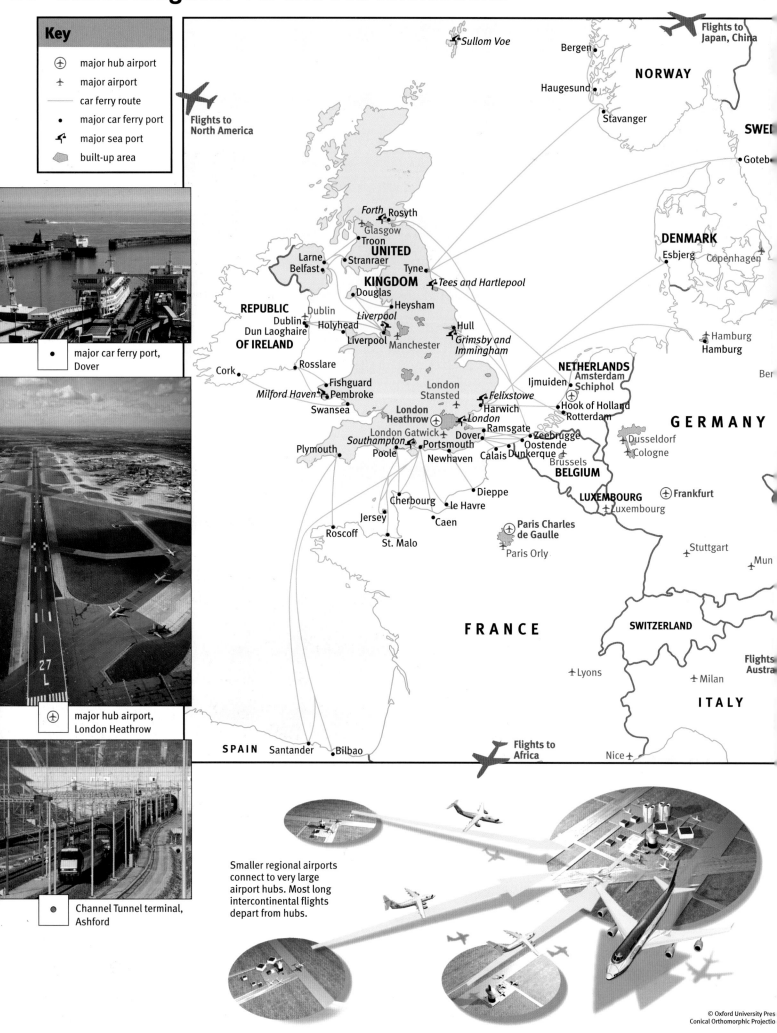

Key

⊕ major hub airport
✈ major airport
— car ferry route
• major car ferry port
⚓ major sea port
⬡ built-up area

major car ferry port,
Dover

⊕ major hub airport,
London Heathrow

⬤ Channel Tunnel terminal,
Ashford

Flights to
North America

Flights to
Japan, China

NORWAY
Bergen
Haugesund
Stavanger

SWE
Goteb

DENMARK
Esbjerg
Copenhagen

Sullom Voe

Forth   Rosyth
Glasgow
Troon
UNITED
Larne   Stranraer   Tyne
Belfast   **KINGDOM**   Tees and Hartlepool
Douglas
Heysham
REPUBLIC   Dublin   Liverpool   Hull
Dublin   Holyhead   Grimsby and
Dun Laoghaire   Liverpool   Immingham
OF IRELAND   Manchester

Cork   Rosslare   London   Stansted   Felixstowe
Fishguard   Harwich
Milford Haven   Pembroke   London   Amsterdam   Ijmuiden
Swansea   Heathrow   London   Schiphol
London Gatwick   Dover   Ramsgate   Hook of Holland
Southampton   Portsmouth   Zeebrugge   Rotterdam
Plymouth   Poole   Newhaven   Calais   Oostende
Dunkerque
Dieppe   Brussels
Cherbourg   le Havre   **BELGIUM**
Jersey   Caen   **LUXEMBOURG**
Roscoff   Luxembourg
St. Malo   Paris Charles
de Gaulle
Paris Orly

NETHERLANDS
GERMANY
Hamburg
Hamburg
Ber
Dusseldorf
Cologne
⊕ Frankfurt
Stuttgart
Mun

FRANCE
SWITZERLAND
ITALY
Lyons   Milan
Flights
Austra
Nice

SPAIN   Santander   Bilbao
Flights to
Africa

Smaller regional airports
connect to very large
airport hubs. Most long
intercontinental flights
depart from hubs.

© Oxford University Pres
Conical Orthomorphic Projectio

Key

- motorway
- major road
- main railway
- ● road or rail terminal
- land over 200m
- land under 200m
- built-up area

Scale One centimetre on the map represents 45 kilometres on the ground.

| 0 | 45 | 90 | 135km |

motorway, M62 near Manchester.

Thurso

Ullapool

Kyle of Lochalsh

Inverness

Aberdeen

Oban

Dundee

Glasgow

Edinburgh

Newcastle upon Tyne

Middlesbrough

Londonderry

Larne

Belfast

Scarborough

Workington

UNITED KINGDOM

Sligo

Blackpool

Bradford

Leeds

Kingston upon Hull

Westport

Liverpool

Manchester

REPUBLIC OF IRELAND

Sheffield

Stoke-on-Trent

Dublin

Holyhead

Nottingham

Norwich

Leicester

Tralee

Birmingham

Rosslare

Coventry

Fishguard

Oxford

Cork

London

Bristol

Ashford

Dover

Folkestone

Calais

Southampton

Brighton

Portsmouth

Weymouth

Penzance

Plymouth

Dieppe

Cherbourg

FRANCE

le Havre

University Press
Mercator Projection

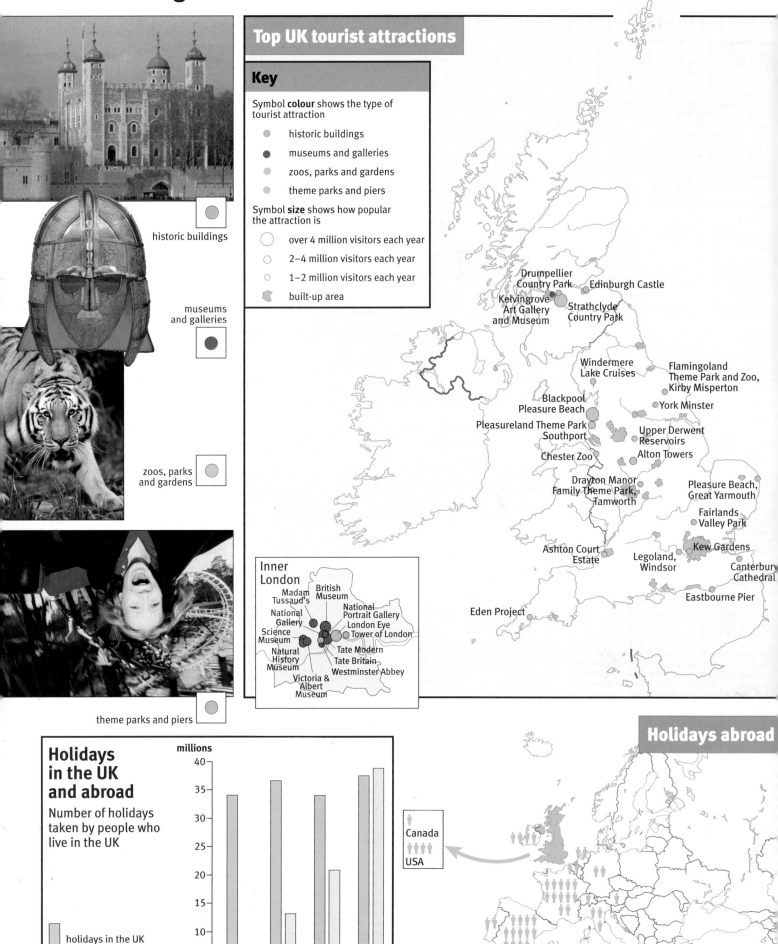

Top UK tourist attractions

Key

Symbol **colour** shows the type of tourist attraction

- historic buildings
- museums and galleries
- zoos, parks and gardens
- theme parks and piers

Symbol **size** shows how popular the attraction is

- over 4 million visitors each year
- 2–4 million visitors each year
- 1–2 million visitors each year
- built-up area

historic buildings

museums and galleries

zoos, parks and gardens

theme parks and piers

Drumpellier Country Park
Edinburgh Castle
Kelvingrove Art Gallery and Museum
Strathclyde Country Park
Windermere Lake Cruises
Flamingoland Theme Park and Zoo, Kirby Misperton
Blackpool Pleasure Beach
York Minster
Pleasureland Theme Park, Southport
Upper Derwent Reservoirs
Chester Zoo
Alton Towers
Drayton Manor Family Theme Park, Tamworth
Pleasure Beach, Great Yarmouth
Fairlands Valley Park
Ashton Court Estate
Legoland, Windsor
Kew Gardens
Canterbury Cathedral
Eden Project
Eastbourne Pier

Inner London

Madam Tussaud's
British Museum
National Gallery
National Portrait Gallery
Science Museum
London Eye
Tower of London
Natural History Museum
Tate Modern
Tate Britain
Victoria & Albert Museum
Westminster Abbey

Holidays abroad

Canada
USA

each symbol stands for 1 million British tourists

Holidays in the UK and abroad

Number of holidays taken by people who live in the UK

millions

- holidays in the UK
- holidays abroad

1971   1981   1991   2001

© Oxford University Press

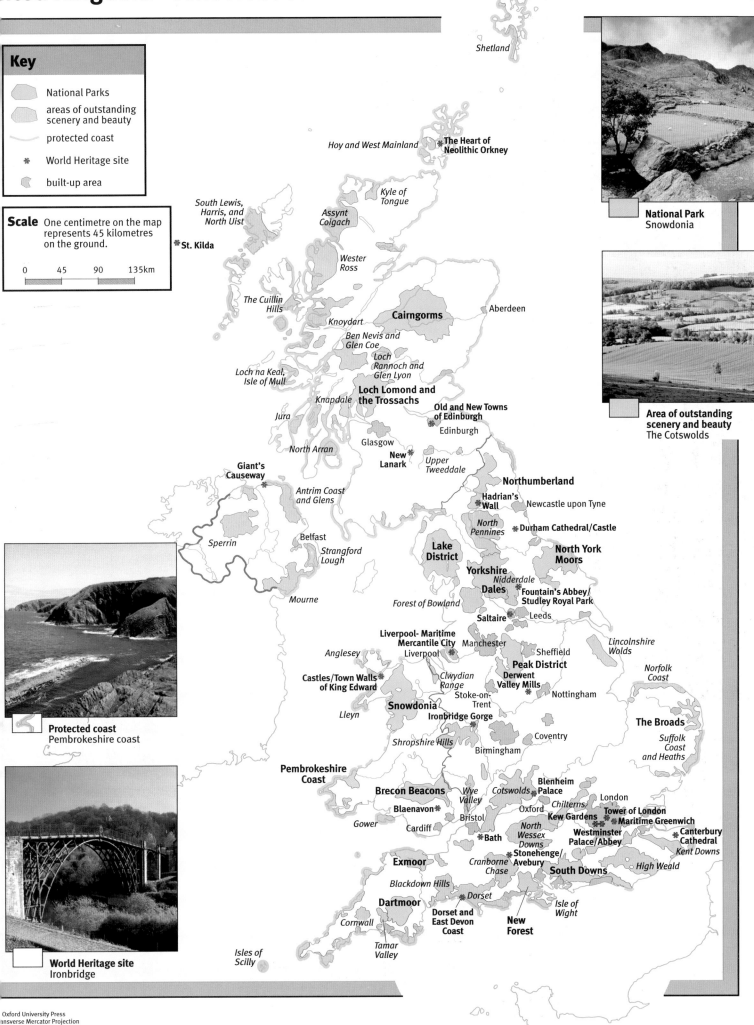

Key

- National Parks
- areas of outstanding scenery and beauty
- protected coast
- ✱ World Heritage site
- built-up area

Scale One centimetre on the map represents 45 kilometres on the ground.

0   45   90   135km

National Park
Snowdonia

Area of outstanding scenery and beauty
The Cotswolds

Protected coast
Pembrokeshire coast

World Heritage site
Ironbridge

Shetland

Hoy and West Mainland ✱ **The Heart of Neolithic Orkney**

South Lewis, Harris, and North Uist

Kyle of Tongue

Assynt Coigach

✱ **St. Kilda**

Wester Ross

The Cuillin Hills

Knoydart

Cairngorms

Aberdeen

Ben Nevis and Glen Coe

Loch Rannoch and Glen Lyon

Loch na Keal, Isle of Mull

Loch Lomond and the Trossachs

Knapdale

Old and New Towns of Edinburgh ✱

Jura

Edinburgh

North Arran

Glasgow

New Lanark ✱

Upper Tweeddale

Giant's Causeway ✱

Antrim Coast and Glens

Northumberland

Hadrian's Wall ✱

Newcastle upon Tyne

Sperrin

Belfast

North Pennines

✱ **Durham Cathedral/Castle**

Strangford Lough

Lake District

North York Moors

Mourne

Yorkshire Dales

Nidderdale

✱ **Fountain's Abbey/ Studley Royal Park**

Forest of Bowland

Saltaire ✱

Leeds

Liverpool- Maritime Mercantile City ✱

Manchester

Lincolnshire Wolds

Anglesey

Liverpool

Sheffield

Norfolk Coast

Peak District

Castles/Town Walls of King Edward ✱

Clwydian Range

Derwent Valley Mills ✱

Nottingham

Lleyn

Snowdonia

Stoke-on-Trent

Ironbridge Gorge ✱

The Broads

Shropshire Hills

Coventry

Birmingham

Suffolk Coast and Heaths

Pembrokeshire Coast

Blenheim Palace ✱

Brecon Beacons

Wye Valley

Cotswolds

London

Blaenavon ✱

Oxford

Chilterns

Tower of London ✱

Kew Gardens ✱

✱ **Maritime Greenwich**

Gower

Bristol

Cardiff

North Wessex Downs

Westminster Palace/Abbey ✱

✱ **Canterbury Cathedral**

✱ **Bath**

✱ **Stonehenge/ Avebury**

Kent Downs

Exmoor

Cranborne Chase

South Downs

High Weald

Blackdown Hills

✱ *Dorset*

Isle of Wight

Dartmoor

Dorset and East Devon Coast

New Forest

Cornwall

Tamar Valley

Isles of Scilly

Oxford University Press
Transverse Mercator Projection

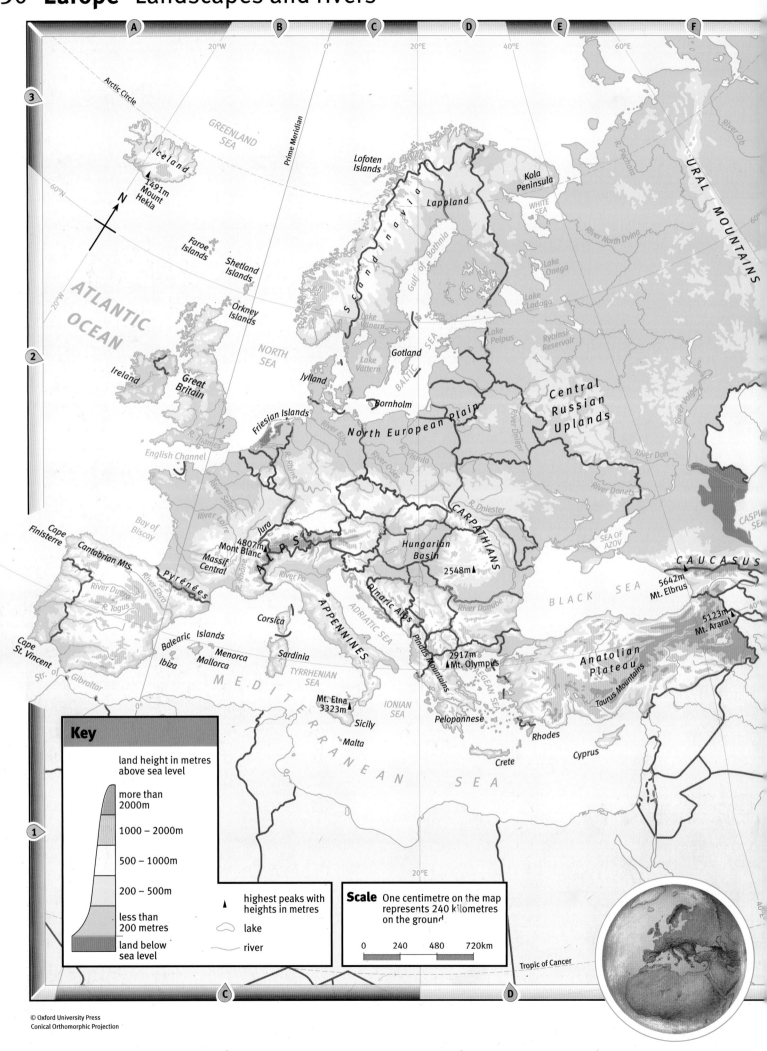

Key

land height in metres above sea level

more than 2000m

1000 – 2000m

500 – 1000m

200 – 500m

less than 200 metres

land below sea level

▲ highest peaks with heights in metres

lake

river

Scale One centimetre on the map represents 240 kilometres on the ground

0   240   480   720km

Arctic Circle

GREENLAND SEA

Iceland
▲1491m Mount Hekla

N

60°N

Faroe Islands

Shetland Islands

Orkney Islands

ATLANTIC OCEAN

Ireland

Great Britain

R. Thames

English Channel

NORTH SEA

Friesian Islands

R. Rhine

Bay of Biscay

River Seine

River Loire

Cape Finisterre

Cantabrian Mts.

Pyrénées

Massif Central

Jura

Mont Blanc 4807m▲

ALPS

R. Rhone

River Po

APPENNINES

Corsica

Balearic Islands

Menorca

Mallorca

Ibiza

Sardinia

TYRRHENIAN SEA

Mt. Etna 3323m▲

Sicily

Malta

River Duero

R. Tagus

River Ebro

Cape St. Vincent

Str. of Gibraltar

M E D I T E R R A N E A N   S E A

Scandinavia

Lofoten Islands

Lappland

Gulf of Bothnia

Lake Vänern

Lake Vättern

Gotland

BALTIC SEA

Bornholm

Jylland

North European Plain

River Elbe

River Oder

R. Vistula

Hungarian Basin

2548m▲

Dinaric Alps

ADRIATIC SEA

Pindus Mountains

2917m ▲Mt. Olympus

AEGEAN SEA

Peloponnese

IONIAN SEA

Crete

Rhodes

Cyprus

CARPATHIANS

River Danube

R. Dniester

River Dniepr

Kola Peninsula

WHITE SEA

River North Dvina

Lake Onega

Lake Ladoga

Lake Peipus

Rybinsk Reservoir

Central Russian Uplands

River Don

River Danets

River Volga

SEA OF AZOV

BLACK SEA

URAL MOUNTAINS

River Pechora

River Ob

CASPIAN SEA

CAUCASUS

5642m▲ Mt. Elbrus

5123m▲ Mt. Ararat

Anatolian Plateau

Taurus Mountains

Tropic of Cancer

© Oxford University Press
Conical Orthomorphic Projection

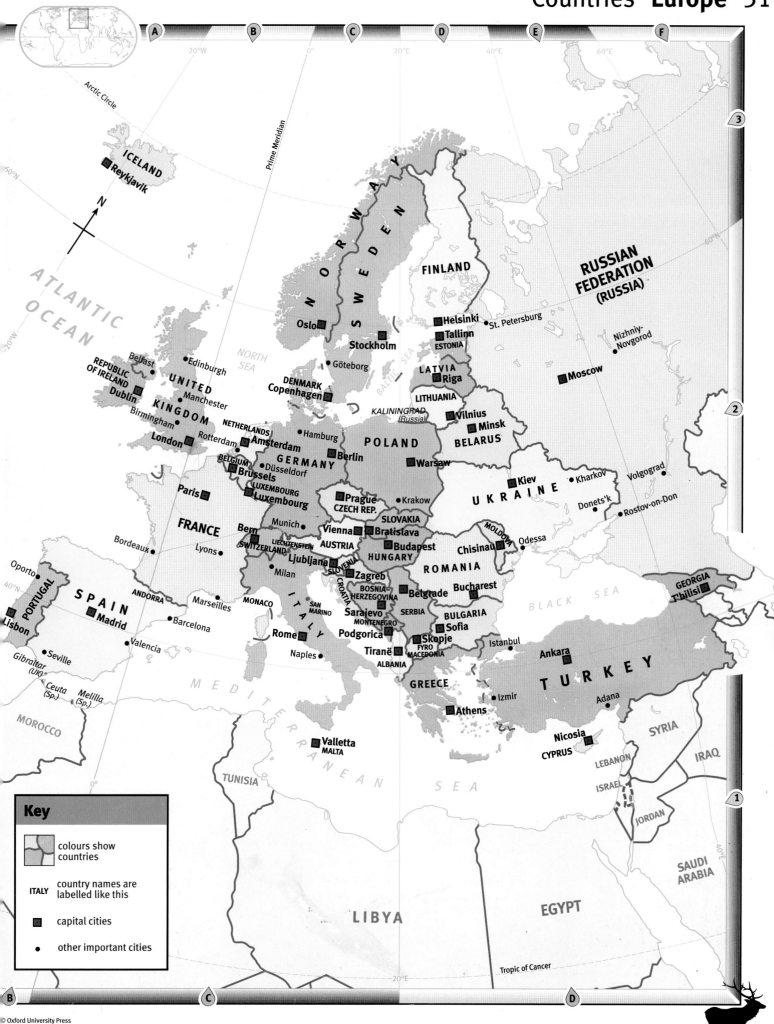

A B C D E F

3

2

1

Arctic Circle

Prime Meridian

ATLANTIC OCEAN

N

ICELAND
■ Reykjavik

NORWAY
SWEDEN
FINLAND

RUSSIAN FEDERATION (RUSSIA)

• St. Petersburg
Helsinki
Tallinn
ESTONIA

• Nizhniy-Novgorod

■ Moscow

Oslo ■

Stockholm ■

• Göteborg

NORTH SEA

LATVIA
Riga

LITHUANIA

KALININGRAD (Russia)

Vilnius
Minsk

BALTIC SEA

Belfast • Edinburgh
REPUBLIC OF IRELAND
Dublin
UNITED KINGDOM
Manchester •
Birmingham •
London ■

DENMARK
Copenhagen ■

NETHERLANDS
Amsterdam ■
• Hamburg
Rotterdam •

BELGIUM
Brussels ■

Paris ■

LUXEMBOURG
Luxembourg ■

GERMANY
Berlin ■
• Düsseldorf

POLAND
Warsaw ■

BELARUS

Kiev ■
• Kharkov
• Volgograd

UKRAINE

Prague ■
CZECH REP.
• Krakow

• Donets'k
• Rostov-on-Don

FRANCE

Munich •

Bern ■
SWITZERLAND
LIECHTENSTEIN

Vienna ■
AUSTRIA

SLOVAKIA
Bratislava ■

MOLDOVA
Chisinau ■
• Odessa

Bordeaux •
Lyons •

Budapest ■
HUNGARY

ROMANIA

Ljubljana ■
SLOVENIA

Milan •

Zagreb ■
CROATIA

Belgrade ■
Bucharest ■

GEORGIA
T'bilisi ■

ANDORRA

Oporto •
PORTUGAL

SPAIN
Madrid ■

• Marseilles

MONACO

ITALY

SAN MARINO

BOSNIA–HERZEGOVINA
Sarajevo ■

SERBIA

BLACK SEA

• Barcelona

Rome ■

Podgorica ■
MONTENEGRO

BULGARIA
Sofia ■

40°N

Lisbon ■

• Valencia

Naples •

Tiranë ■
ALBANIA

Skopje ■
FYRO MACEDONIA

• Istanbul

Ankara ■

Gibraltar (UK)

• Seville

GREECE

• Izmir

TURKEY

• Adana

Ceuta (Sp.)
Melilla (Sp.)

MOROCCO

Athens ■

Valletta ■
MALTA

MEDITERRANEAN

SEA

Nicosia ■
CYPRUS

SYRIA
LEBANON

IRAQ

TUNISIA

ISRAEL
JORDAN

SAUDI ARABIA

LIBYA

EGYPT

Tropic of Cancer

20°W 20°W 0° 20°E 40°E 60°E

50°N 60°N

40°N 40°E

0° 20°E

Key

colours show countries

ITALY country names are labelled like this

■ capital cities

• other important cities

32 Europe

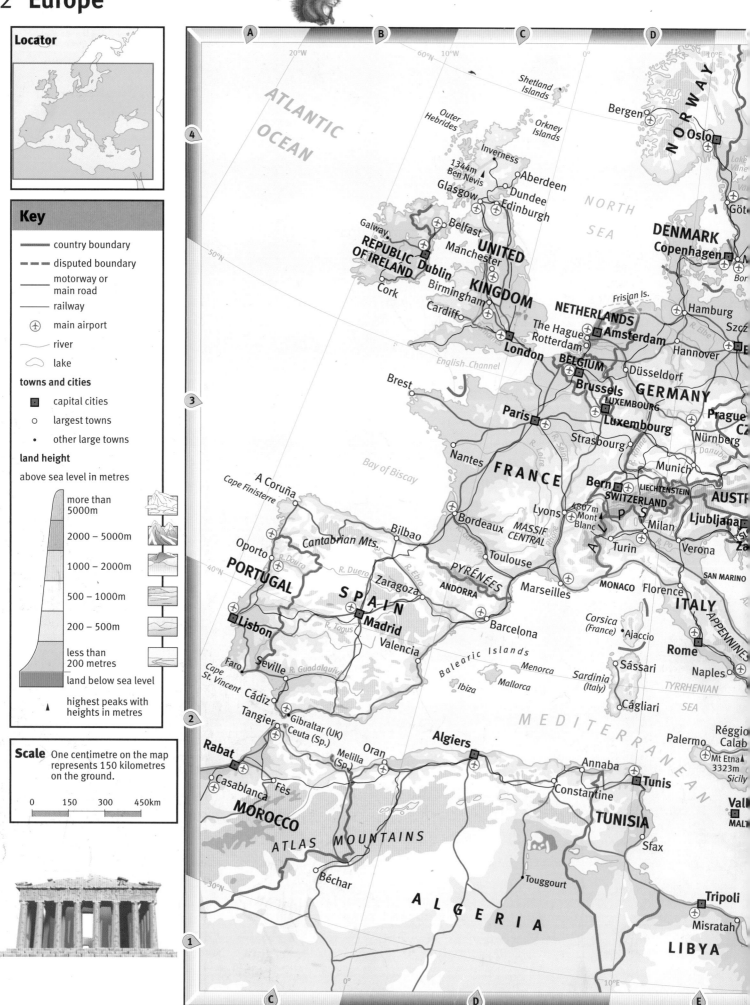

Locator

Key

— country boundary
--- disputed boundary
— motorway or
main road
— railway
⊕ main airport
〜 river
⌓ lake

towns and cities
■ capital cities
○ largest towns
• other large towns

land height
above sea level in metres

more than 5000m
2000 – 5000m
1000 – 2000m
500 – 1000m
200 – 500m
less than 200 metres
land below sea level
▲ highest peaks with heights in metres

Scale One centimetre on the map represents 150 kilometres on the ground.

0   150   300   450km

ATLANTIC OCEAN

20°W   60°W   10°W   0°   10°E

Shetland Islands
Outer Hebrides
Orkney Islands

Bergen
NORWAY
Oslo

NORTH SEA

1344m Ben Nevis
Inverness
Aberdeen
Glasgow
Dundee
Edinburgh
Belfast
Galway
Manchester
UNITED KINGDOM
Dublin
REPUBLIC OF IRELAND
Cork
Birmingham
Cardiff
London
Brest

DENMARK
Copenhagen
Göt
Bor

Frisian Is.
NETHERLANDS
The Hague
Rotterdam
Amsterdam
BELGIUM
Brussels
LUXEMBOURG
Luxembourg
Düsseldorf
GERMANY
Hamburg
Szcz
Hannover
Prague
CZ
Nürnberg
Danube

English Channel

50°N

Paris
Strasbourg
Nantes
FRANCE
Bern
SWITZERLAND
LIECHTENSTEIN
AUSTR
Ljubljana

Bay of Biscay

A Coruña
Cape Finisterre
Oporto
R. Douro
PORTUGAL
Lisbon
Faro
Cape St. Vincent
Cádiz
Seville
R. Guadalquivir
SPAIN
Madrid
Valencia
R. Tagus
R. Duero
Zaragoza
Bilbao
Cantabrian Mts.
Bordeaux
Toulouse
PYRÉNÉES
ANDORRA
Barcelona
Marseilles
MASSIF CENTRAL
Lyons
4807m Mont Blanc
ALPS
Milan
Turin
Verona
MONACO
SAN MARINO
Florence
ITALY
Rome
APPENNINES
Za

40°N

Balearic Islands
Menorca
Mallorca
Ibiza
Corsica (France)
Ajaccio
Sardinia (Italy)
Sássari
Cágliari
Naples
TYRRHENIAN SEA
Palermo
Réggio Calab
Mt Etna 3323m
Sicily

MEDITERRANEAN

Tangier
Gibraltar (UK)
Ceuta (Sp.)
Melilla (Sp.)
Oran
Algiers
Annaba
Tunis
TUNISIA
Constantine
Rabat
Casablanca
Fès
MOROCCO
ATLAS MOUNTAINS
Sfax

30°N

Béchar
ALGERIA
Touggourt
Tripoli
Misrath
LIBYA
Val
MAL

0°   10°E

A   B   C   D

4   3   2   1

C   D   E

FINLAND

Lake Onega

Helsinki

St. Petersburg

Vologda

Lake Ladoga

Stockholm

Tallinn

ESTONIA

Lake Peipus

Rybinsk Reservoir

Nizhniy-Novgorod Kazan'

R. Volga

Samara

Gotland

G. of Riga

LATVIA

Riga

Moscow

RUSSIAN FEDERATION
(RUSSIA)

Kaliningrad

RUSSIA

LITHUANIA

Vilnius

Minsk

BELARUS

R. Dnieper

sk

European Plain

R. Don

POLAND

roclaw

Warsaw

Kiev

UKRAINE

Kharkov

Volgograd

Krakow

L'viv

R. Dniester

Dnipropetrovsk

Donets'k

Rostov-on-Don

SLOVAKIA

Bratislava

CARPATHIANS

MOLDOVA

Chisinau

Odessa

Crimea

SEA OF AZOV

Mt. Elbrus 5642m

na

dapest

HUNGARY

ROMANIA

Sevastopol

CAUCASUS MTS

GEORGIA

SNIA-RZEGOVINA

Belgrade

Bucharest

Constanta

R. Danube

BLACK SEA

Sarajevo

SERBIA

Sofia

BULGARIA

Samsun

ALPS

NTENEGRO

dgorica

Skopje

FYRO MACEDONIA

Istanbul

Sivas

Tiranë

ALBANIA

Thessaloníki

Mt. Olympus 2917m

Ankara

TURKEY

Kayseri

aranto

Bursa

Konya

Adana

Taurus Mountains

Aleppo

R. Euphrates

GREECE

PINDUS MTS

Izmir

AEGEAN SEA

IONIAN SEA

Athens

Peloponnese

Rhodes

Nicosia

CYPRUS

SYRIA

Iraklión

LEBANON

Beirut

Damascus

Crete

SEA

ISRAEL

Amman

Jerusalem

Dead Sea

JORDAN

Benghazi

Alexandria

Port Said

Sinai

EGYPT

El Giza

Cairo

SAUDI ARABIA

Bridges over the River Seine in Paris

Bridges over the
River Vltava in Prague

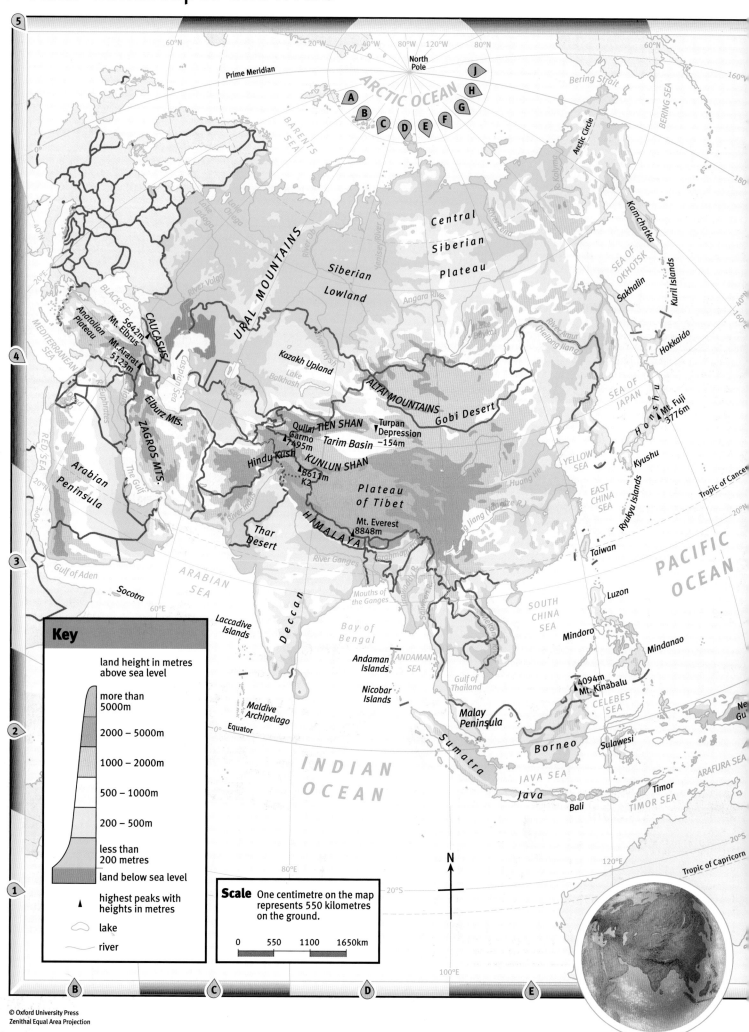

Key

land height in metres above sea level

more than 5000m

2000 – 5000m

1000 – 2000m

500 – 1000m

200 – 500m

less than 200 metres

land below sea level

▲ highest peaks with heights in metres

lake

river

Scale One centimetre on the map represents 550 kilometres on the ground.

0   550   1100   1650km

N

© Oxford University Press
Zenithal Equal Area Projection

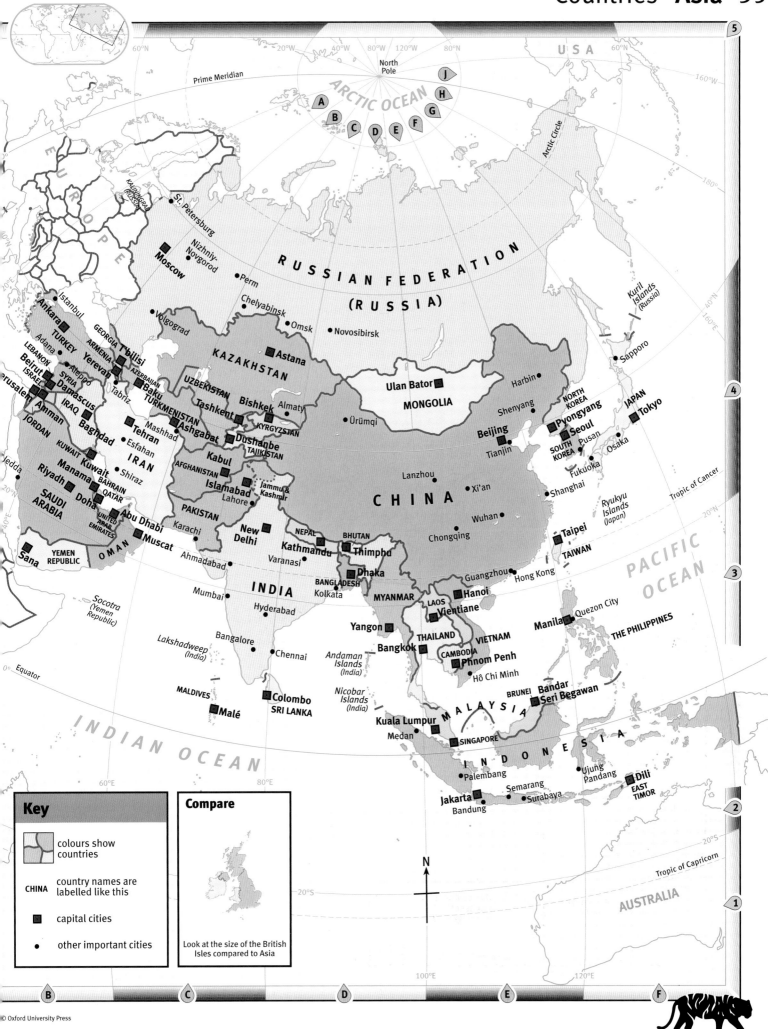

5

60°N 20°W 40°W 80°W 120°W 80°N USA 60°N

North Pole

Prime Meridian

ARCTIC OCEAN

Ⓐ Ⓑ Ⓒ Ⓓ Ⓔ Ⓕ Ⓖ Ⓗ Ⓙ

160°W

Arctic Circle

180°

160°E

40°N

St. Petersburg

Nizhniy-Novgorod

Moscow

Perm

Chelyabinsk

RUSSIAN FEDERATION

(RUSSIA)

Kuril Islands (Russia)

Sapporo

4

Volgograd

Omsk

Novosibirsk

Istanbul

Ankara

TURKEY

GEORGIA T'bilisi

ARMENIA Yerevan

Adana

Aleppo

LEBANON

SYRIA

Beirut

Damascus

Tabriz

AZERBAIJAN

Baku

TURKMENISTAN

KAZAKHSTAN

Astana

UZBEKISTAN

Tashkent

Bishkek

Almaty

Ürümqi

MONGOLIA

Ulan Bator

Harbin

Shenyang

NORTH KOREA

Pyongyang

Seoul

JAPAN

Tokyo

ISRAEL

Jerusalem

IRAQ

Amman

JORDAN

Baghdad

KUWAIT

Kuwait

Tehran

Mashhad

Ashgabat

Dushanbe

TAJIKISTAN

Kabul

AFGHANISTAN

Islamabad

Jammu & Kashmir

Lahore

Beijing

Tianjin

SOUTH KOREA

Pusan

Fukuoka

Osaka

Tropic of Cancer

Esfahan

IRAN

Shiraz

Lanzhou

Xi'an

CHINA

Ryukyu Islands (Japan)

20°N

Jedda

Manama

BAHRAIN

Riyadh

Doha

QATAR

SAUDI ARABIA

UNITED ARAB EMIRATES

Abu Dhabi

Muscat

OMAN

PAKISTAN

Karachi

New Delhi

NEPAL

Kathmandu

BHUTAN

Thimphu

Ahmadabad

Chongqing

Wuhan

Shanghai

Taipei

TAIWAN

Guangzhou

Hong Kong

PACIFIC OCEAN

3

Sana

YEMEN REPUBLIC

Socotra (Yemen Republic)

Mumbai

INDIA

Hyderabad

Dhaka

BANGLADESH

Kolkata

MYANMAR

Yangon

LAOS

Hanoi

Vientiane

Manila

Quezon City

THE PHILIPPINES

Lakshadweep (India)

Bangalore

Chennai

Andaman Islands (India)

THAILAND

Bangkok

CAMBODIA

VIETNAM

Phnom Penh

Hô Chi Minh

0° Equator

MALDIVES

Malé

Colombo

SRI LANKA

Nicobar Islands (India)

BRUNEI

Bandar Seri Begawan

MALAYSIA

INDIA OCEAN

Kuala Lumpur

Medan

SINGAPORE

INDONESIA

Palembang

Semarang

Ujung Pandang

Dili

EAST TIMOR

60°E 80°E

Jakarta

Bandung

Surabaya

2

20°S

Key

colours show countries

CHINA country names are labelled like this

■ capital cities

• other important cities

Compare

Look at the size of the British Isles compared to Asia

N

100°E

Tropic of Capricorn

20°S

AUSTRALIA

1

Ⓑ Ⓒ Ⓓ Ⓔ Ⓕ

© Oxford University Press

Key

——	country boundary
- - -	disputed boundary
——	motorway or main road
——	railway
✈	main airport
∿	river
◡	lake

land height

above sea level in metres

- more than 5000m
- 2000 – 5000m
- 1000 – 2000m
- 500 – 1000m
- 200 – 500m
- less than 200 metres
- land below sea level
- ▲ highest peaks with heights in metres

towns and cities

- ▣ capital cities
- ○ largest towns
- • other large towns

Scale One centimetre on the map represents 125 kilometres on the ground.

0   125   250   375km

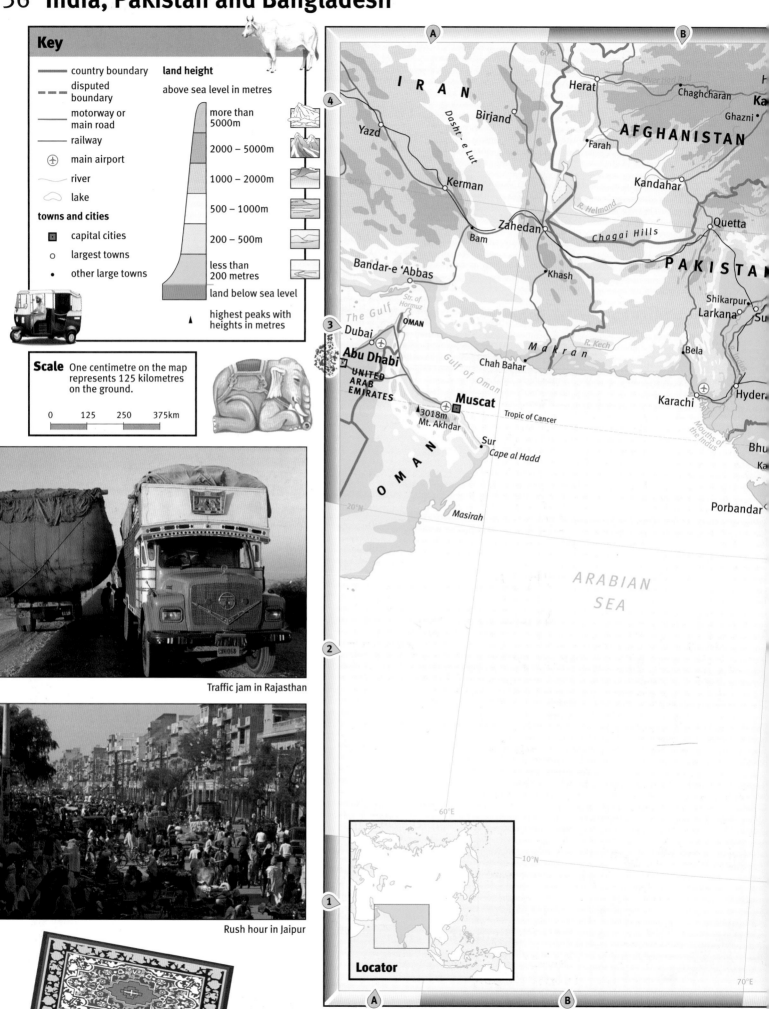

Traffic jam in Rajasthan

Rush hour in Jaipur

IRAN
Herat, Birjand, Yazd, Kerman, Bam, Zahedan

AFGHANISTAN
Chaghcharan, Ka, Ghazni, Farah, Kandahar, R. Helmand, Chagai Hills, Khash

PAKISTAN
Quetta, Shikarpur, Larkana, Su, Bela, Karachi, Hyder..., Bhu, Ka

Bandar-e 'Abbas, Str. of Hormuz, The Gulf, Dubai, **OMAN**, Abu Dhabi, **UNITED ARAB EMIRATES**, Gulf of Oman, Makran, R. Kech, Chah Bahar

Muscat, ▲3018m Mt. Akhdar, Tropic of Cancer, Mouths of the Indus

OMAN, Sur, Cape al Hadd, Masirah, 20°N, Porbandar

ARABIAN SEA

60°E, 10°N, 70°E

Locator

© Oxford University Press
Conical Orthomorphic Projection

PAMIRS
TAJIKISTAN
Khorog

7690m

Gilgit

K2 (Qogir Feng,
Godwin Austen)
8611m

Rutog

C H I N A

awar

Srinagar

Leh

Islamabad
Rawalpindi

JAMMU
AND
KASHMIR

Jammu

Gujranwala

Lahore   Amritsar

isalabad

Chandigarh

Multan
Ghazi Khan

Ludhiana

River Sutlej

Dehra Dun

Lhasa

Nyingchi

Bahawalpur

R. Yamuna

Meerut

yar

Desert

Bikaner

New Delhi   Delhi

R. Ghaghara

Bareilly

8091m
Annapurna

Mount
Everest
8848m

Lhaze

Thimphu
BHUTAN

Dibrugarh

Brahmaputra R.

jodhpur

Jaipur

Agra

Lucknow

Gorakhpur

Kathmandu

Darjiling

Guwahati

Nagaon

Shillong

N   E   P   A   L

H I M A L A Y A

Kanpur

Gwalior

River Ganges

R. Chambal

R. Banas

Jhansi

Allahabad

Varanasi

R. Son

Patna
Bhagalpur

Muzaffarpur

BANGLADESH

Imphal

River Chindwin

Kota

I   N   D   I   A

Murwara

R. Ganges

Dhanbad

Asanol

Dhaka

Tropic of Cancer

Gandhi
Sagar

Ahmadabad

Bhopal

Jabalpur

Jamshedpur

Kolkata

Khulna

Chittagong

Monywa

Vadodara   Indore

R. Narmada

Bilaspur

Hirakud
Reservoir

Kharagpur

Mandalay

MYANMAR
(BURMA)

Bharuch

R. Tapi

Raipur

Sambalpur

R. Mahanadi

agar

Surat

Burhanpur

Nagpur

Dhule   Amravati

Cuttack

Sittwe

Arakan Yoma

Nashik

R. Godavari

Aurangabad

Chandrapur

R. Indravati

Brahmapur

Pye

Sandoway

mbai

Pune

Nizamabad

D e c c a n

R. Bhima

Solapur

R. Krishna

Hyderabad

Vishakhapatnam

Bay
of
Bengal

Yangon

Bassein

Mouths of
the Irrawaddy

Kolhapur   Bijapur

Raichur

Rajahmundry

Vijayawada

Belgaum

Bellary

E A S T E R N   G H A T S

R. Pennar

Nellore

W E S T E R N   G H A T S

Andaman
Islands

Mangalore

Bangalore

Vellore

Chennai

Mysore

Pondicherry

Port Blair

Calicut

Salem

ANDAMAN

Coimbatore   Tiruchchirappalli

SEA

Cochin

Madurai

Jaffna

I   N   D   I   A   N   O   C   E   A   N

10°N

Quilon

Trivandrum

SRI LANKA

Trincomalee

Nagercoil

Puttalam

Batticaloa

Laccadive
Islands

Colombo

Kandy

90°E

Badulla

80°E

Galle

Oxford University Press

awar

R. Jhelum

R. Chenab

Peshawar

R. Indus

C D E
4

E
3

E
2

E
1

C D E

A · B · C · D · E

RUSSIAN FEDERATION (RUSSIA)

80°E · 90°E · 100°E · 110°

Pavlodar
Barnaul
Astana
Biysk
River Ob
Karaganda
Semipalatinsk
Rubtsovsk
Lake Baykal
Angarsk · Irkutsk
Ulan-Ude
Chita
50°N
Ust'-Kamenogorsk
Lake Zaysan
Zyryanovsk
Yenisey River
Hövsgöl Nuur
Borzya
KAZAKHSTAN
Ayaguz
Altay
Ulaangom
Manzhouli
Lake Balkhash
Taldykorgan
Hovd
Selenge River
Choybalsan
Lake Alakol
MONGOLIA
Ulan Bator
Almaty
Yining
ALTAI MOUNTAINS
Gobi Desert
Saynshand
Bishkek
Ürümqi
KYRGYZSTAN
TIEN SHAN
Turpan
Hami
Erenhot
Turpan Depression −154m
Kashi
Hohhot · Jining · Zhangjia
Tarim He
Lop Nur
Baotou
Datong · Tangs
Tarim Pendi
Anxi
Wuhai
Tianj
Yumen
Qilian Shan
Yinchuan
Great Wall
Shijiazh
K2 (Qogir Feng) 8611m
Altun Shan
Taiyuan
Dezhou
Kunlun Shan
C
Golmud
Xining
Lanzhou
Handan · inar
JAMMU AND KASHMIR
H
I
N
A
Changzhi
Rutog
Baoji
Zhengzhou
3
Plateau of Tibet
Chang Jiang
Xuzhe
Luoyang
Xi'an
Suzho
Dehra Dun
300
Xiangfan
Beng
He
Bareilly
NEPAL
Chengdu
Chang Jiang (Yangtze River)
Wuhar
Annapurna 8091m
Lhaze
Lhasa
Chongqing
Donting Po Hu
Jingd
Lucknow
Kathmandu
Darjiling
Batang
Neijiang
Changde
Nanchan
Kanpur
Gorakhpur
THIMPHU
Dibrugarh
Yibin
Changsha
Zhuzhou
Allahabad · Varanasi
Muzaffarpur
BHUTAN
Brahmaputra R.
Zunyi
Guiyang · Shaoyang
Hengyang
Murwara
Patna
Bhagalpur
Shillong
Dali
Duyun
Gan
Tropic of Cancer
Dhanbad
BANGLADESH
Imphal
R. Chindwin
Kunming
Guilin
Nan Ling
Shaogua
Jabalpur
Jamshedpur
Dhaka
Liuzhou
Wuzhou
INDIA
Khulna
Chittagong
Monywa
Song Koi
Nanning
Guangz
Bilaspur
Kharagpur
Kolkata
Lao Cai
Macao · Hong
Raipur
Mouths of the Ganges
MYANMAR
Shweli R.
Pingxiang
Cuttack
Mandalay
Mekong R.
Phongsali
Zhanjiang
20°N
(BURMA)
Kengtung
Hanoi
Hai Phong
Brahmapur
Arakan Yoma
Sittwe
Thanh Hoa
Haikou
1
Vishakhapatnam
Chiang Mai
Louangphrabang
Vinh
Hainan Dao
Bay of Bengal
Pye
Vientiane
Udon Thani
SOU
CHI
SE
Bassein
Pegu
THAILAND
Huê
Da Nang
Yangon
Moulmein
Mouths of the Irrawaddy
100°E
110°E

90°E

A · B · C · D · E

© Oxford University Pres
Conical Orthomorphic Projection

Map labels (China, Japan, Korea, Taiwan, Philippines region):

River Amur · Komsomol'sk-na-Amure · Sakhalin · SEA OF OKHOTSK
Blagoveshchensk · Khabarovsk · Yuzhno-Sakhalinsk · occupied by Russia
Nenjiang · Bei'an · Hegang · Jiamusi · Wakkanai
Qiqihar · Shuangyashan · Jixi · Asahikawa · Kushiro
Daqing · Harbin · Mudanjiang · Otaru · Sapporo · Hokkaido
...heng · Changchun · Jilin · Vladivostok · Hakodate
Siping · Tonghua · Sikhote-Alin' · Lake Khanka
...henyang · Fushun · Chongjin · Aomori · Hachinohe
Anshan · NORTH KOREA · Kimchaek · Akita · Morioka
...uangdao · Dandong · Hamhung · SEA OF JAPAN · Sendai
Korea Bay · Pyongyang · Niigata
Dalian · Kangnung · Tokyo · Yokohama · Kawasaki
Yantai · Inchon · Seoul · SOUTH KOREA · Tottori · Kyoto · Nagoya · 3776m Mt. Fuji
Qingdao · Taejon · Pohang · Kobe · Osaka
YELLOW SEA · Taegu · Pusan · Hiroshima · Kochi
...nyungang · Kwangju · Kita-Kyushu · Shikoku
...ngjiang · Korea Strait · Fukuoka
Cheju do · Nagasaki · Kyushu · Miyazaki
...ng · Changzhou · Kagoshima
EAST CHINA SEA · Ryukyu Islands
...uxi · Shanghai · PACIFIC OCEAN
...zhou · Ningbo
Wenzhou · Okinawa · Tropic of Cancer
...ping · Fuzhou · Taipei · Taichung
...en · Tainan · TAIWAN
...aohsiung
Luzon Strait
Laoag · Luzon · THE PHILIPPINES
Dagupan · Manila · Quezon City

Locator

Mt. Fuji is Japan's highest peak

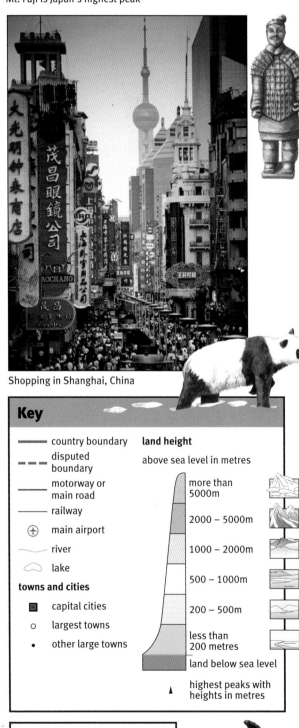

Shopping in Shanghai, China

Key

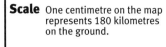

— country boundary
--- disputed boundary
— motorway or main road
— railway
⊕ main airport
∼ river
⌒ lake

towns and cities
■ capital cities
○ largest towns
• other large towns

land height
above sea level in metres

more than 5000m
2000 – 5000m
1000 – 2000m
500 – 1000m
200 – 500m
less than 200 metres
land below sea level

▲ highest peaks with heights in metres

Scale One centimetre on the map represents 180 kilometres on the ground.

0   180   360   540km

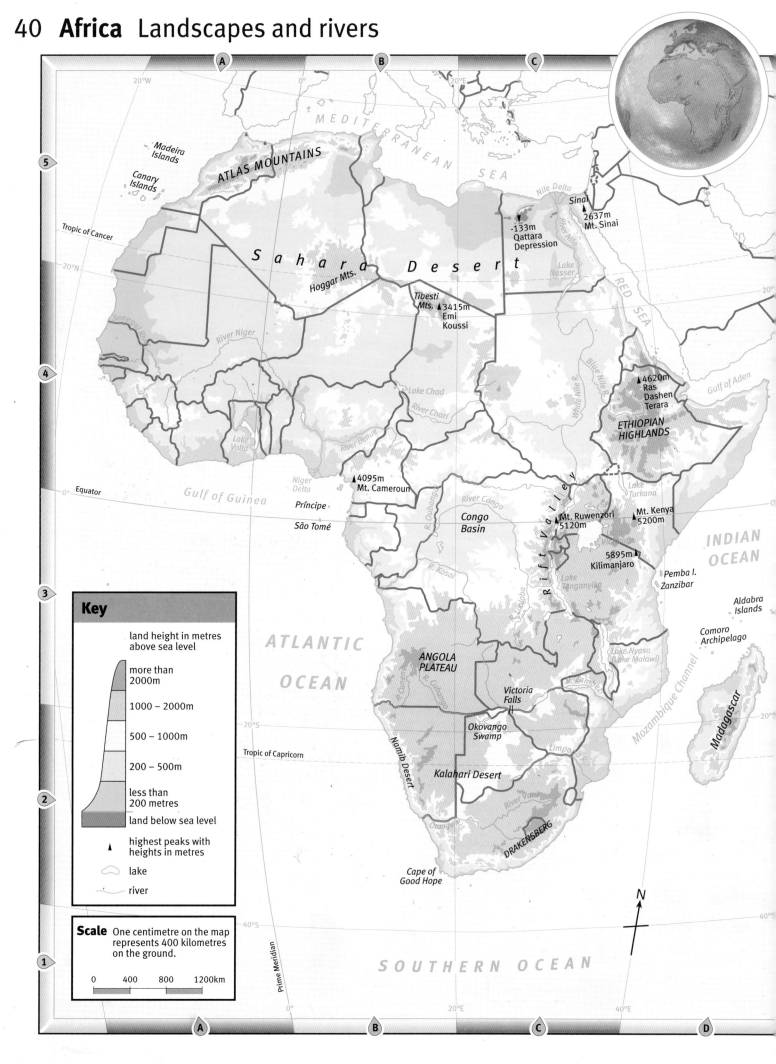

MEDITERRANEAN SEA

Madeira Islands

Canary Islands

ATLAS MOUNTAINS

Tropic of Cancer

20°N

S a h a r a   D e s e r t

Hoggar Mts.

Senegal R.

River Niger

Tibesti Mts. ▲3415m Emi Koussi

Nile Delta

Sinai

-133m Qattara Depression

▲2637m Mt. Sinai

River Nile

Lake Nasser

RED SEA

20°

Lake Chad

River Chari

River Benue

Lake Volta

White Nile R.

Blue Nile R.

▲4620m Ras Dashen Terara

ETHIOPIAN HIGHLANDS

Gulf of Aden

Equator

Gulf of Guinea

Niger Delta

▲4095m Mt. Cameroun

Príncipe

São Tomé

R. Oubangui

River Congo

Congo Basin

Rift Valley

Lake Turkana

Mt. Ruwenzori ▲5120m

Mt. Kenya ▲5200m

INDIAN OCEAN

R. Kasai

5895m▲ Kilimanjaro

Pemba I.
Zanzibar

Aldabra Islands

Comoro Archipelago

R. Lualaba

Lake Tanganyika

ATLANTIC OCEAN

ANGOLA PLATEAU

R. Cuanza

R. Cunene

R. Cubango

Lake Nyasa (Lake Malawi)

R. Zambezi

Mozambique Channel

Madagascar

Victoria Falls

Okovango Swamp

Limpopo R.

20°S

Tropic of Capricorn

Namib Desert

Kalahari Desert

River Vaal

Orange R.

DRAKENSBERG

Cape of Good Hope

N

40°S

SOUTHERN OCEAN

Key

land height in metres above sea level

- more than 2000m
- 1000 – 2000m
- 500 – 1000m
- 200 – 500m
- less than 200 metres
- land below sea level

▲ highest peaks with heights in metres

◠ lake

~ river

Scale One centimetre on the map represents 400 kilometres on the ground.

0   400   800   1200km

20°W

20°E

Prime Meridian

20°E

40°E

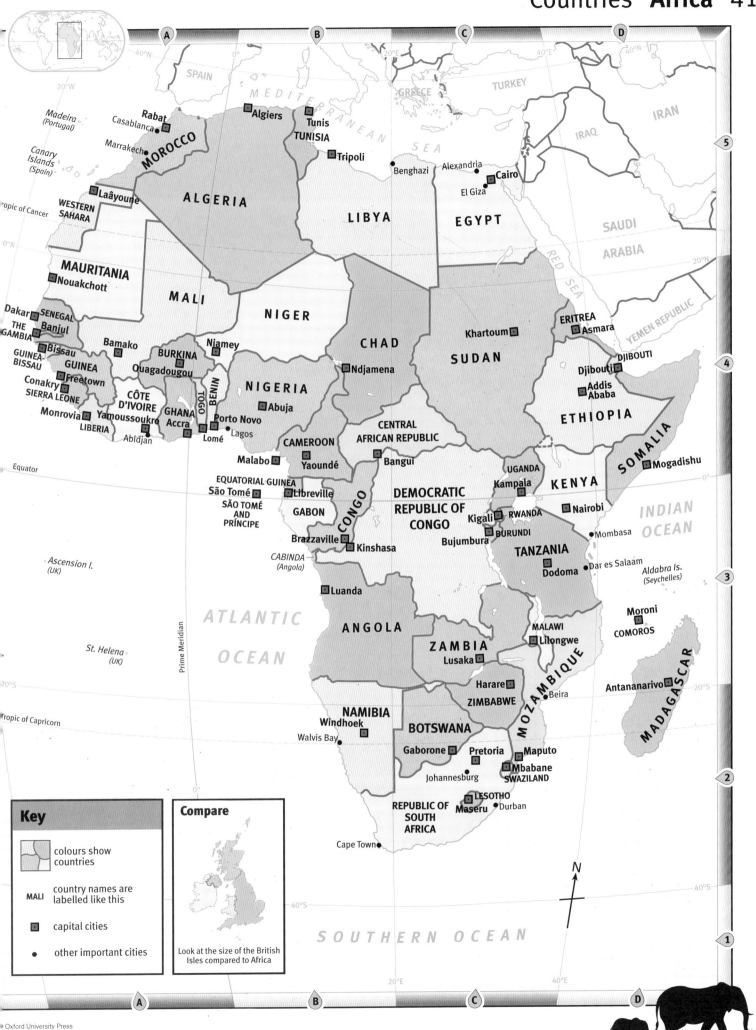

SPAIN

Madeira
(Portugal)

Canary
Islands
(Spain)

Tropic of Cancer

MEDITERRANEAN SEA

GREECE

TURKEY

IRAQ

IRAN

Rabat ■
Casablanca •
Marrakech •
MOROCCO

■ Algiers
Tunis ■
TUNISIA
■ Tripoli

Benghazi •
Alexandria •
■ Cairo
El Giza •

SAUDI
ARABIA

Laâyoune ■
**WESTERN
SAHARA**

ALGERIA

LIBYA

EGYPT

RED SEA

0°N

20°N

MAURITANIA
■ Nouakchott

MALI

NIGER

CHAD

Khartoum ■

SUDAN

ERITREA
■ Asmara

YEMEN REPUBLIC

DJIBOUTI
Djibouti ■

Dakar ■
SENEGAL
THE
GAMBIA
Banjul ■
Bissau ■
**GUINEA-
BISSAU**
Bamako ■
BURKINA
Ouagadougou ■
Niamey ■

GUINEA
Conakry ■
Freetown ■
SIERRA LEONE

**CÔTE
D'IVOIRE**
Monrovia ■
LIBERIA
Yamoussoukro ■
Abidjan •

GHANA
Accra ■
TOGO
Lomé ■

BENIN
Porto Novo ■
Lagos •

NIGERIA
Abuja ■

Ndjamena ■

CAMEROON
Malabo ■
Yaoundé ■

**CENTRAL
AFRICAN REPUBLIC**
Bangui ■

Addis
Ababa ■
ETHIOPIA

SOMALIA
■ Mogadishu

Equator

EQUATORIAL GUINEA
São Tomé ■
**SÃO TOMÉ
AND
PRÍNCIPE**

Libreville ■
GABON
CONGO
Brazzaville ■

**DEMOCRATIC
REPUBLIC OF
CONGO**
Kinshasa ■

UGANDA
Kampala ■
Kigali ■ **RWANDA**
BURUNDI
Bujumbura ■

KENYA
■ Nairobi
Mombasa •

INDIAN
OCEAN

0°

*CABINDA
(Angola)*

TANZANIA
Dodoma ■
Dar es Salaam •

*Aldabra Is.
(Seychelles)*

*Ascension I.
(UK)*

ATLANTIC

OCEAN

Luanda ■

ANGOLA

ZAMBIA
Lusaka ■

MALAWI
Lilongwe ■

Moroni ■
COMOROS

MOZAMBIQUE

20°S

*St. Helena
(UK)*

Prime Meridian

Harare ■
ZIMBABWE
Beira •

Antananarivo ■

MADAGASCAR

Tropic of Capricorn

0°

NAMIBIA
Windhoek ■
Walvis Bay •

BOTSWANA
Gaborone ■

Pretoria ■
Johannesburg •
**REPUBLIC OF
SOUTH
AFRICA**
Cape Town •

Maputo ■
Mbabane ■
SWAZILAND
LESOTHO
Maseru ■ Durban •

40°S

Key

colours show
countries

MALI country names are
labelled like this

■ capital cities

• other important cities

Compare

Look at the size of the British
Isles compared to Africa

N

SOUTHERN OCEAN

20°E

40°E

40°S

Oxford University Press

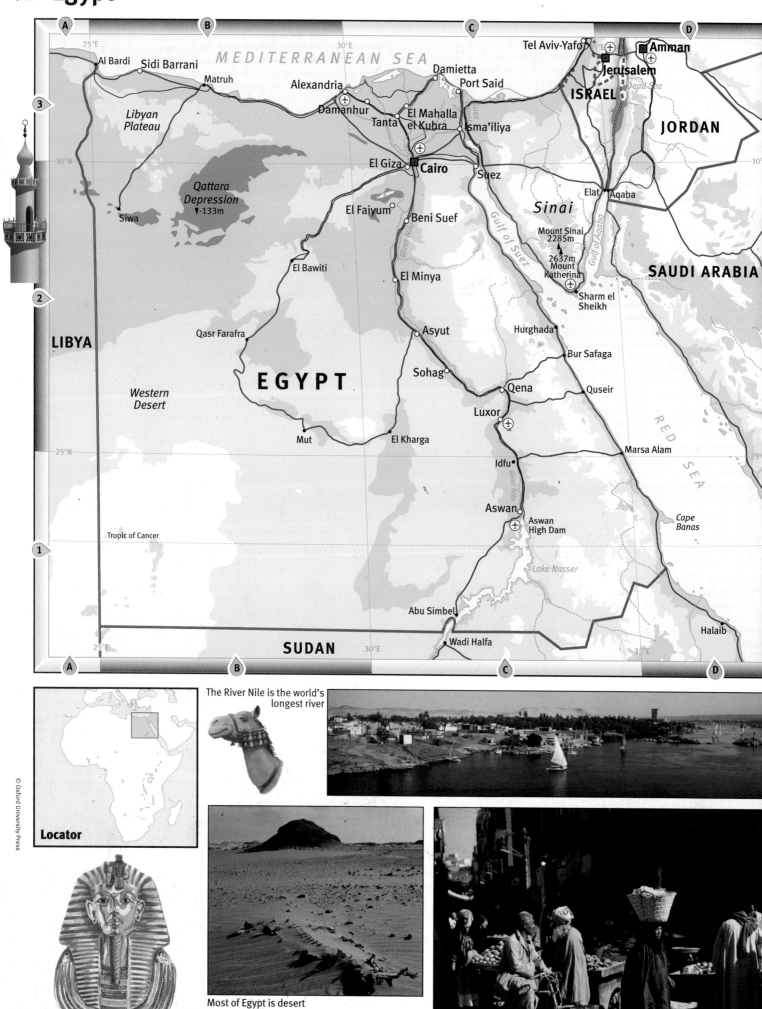

The River Nile is the world's longest river

Most of Egypt is desert

Shopping in the old city, Cairo

Locator

Map labels:

MEDITERRANEAN SEA

Al Bardi, Sidi Barrani, Matruh, Libyan Plateau, Alexandria, Damietta, Port Said, Tel Aviv-Yafo, Amman, Jerusalem, ISRAEL, JORDAN, Damanhur, El Mahalla el Kubra, Tanta, Isma'iliya, El Giza, Cairo, Suez, Elat, Aqaba, Qattara Depression ▼-133m, Siwa, Sinai, El Faiyum, Beni Suef, Mount Sinai 2285m, 2637m Mount Katherina, SAUDI ARABIA, El Bawiti, El Minya, Sharm el Sheikh, Qasr Farafra, Asyut, Hurghada, EGYPT, Sohag, Bur Safaga, Western Desert, Qena, Quseir, Luxor, Mut, El Kharga, Idfu, Marsa Alam, RED SEA, Aswan, Aswan High Dam, Cape Banas, Tropic of Cancer, Lake Nasser, LIBYA, Abu Simbel, Halaib, SUDAN, Wadi Halfa

Coordinates: 25°E, 30°E, 35°E, 30°N, 30°N, 25°N, 25°N, 25°E, 30°E, 35°E

River Nile, Gulf of Suez, Gulf of Aqaba, Dead Sea

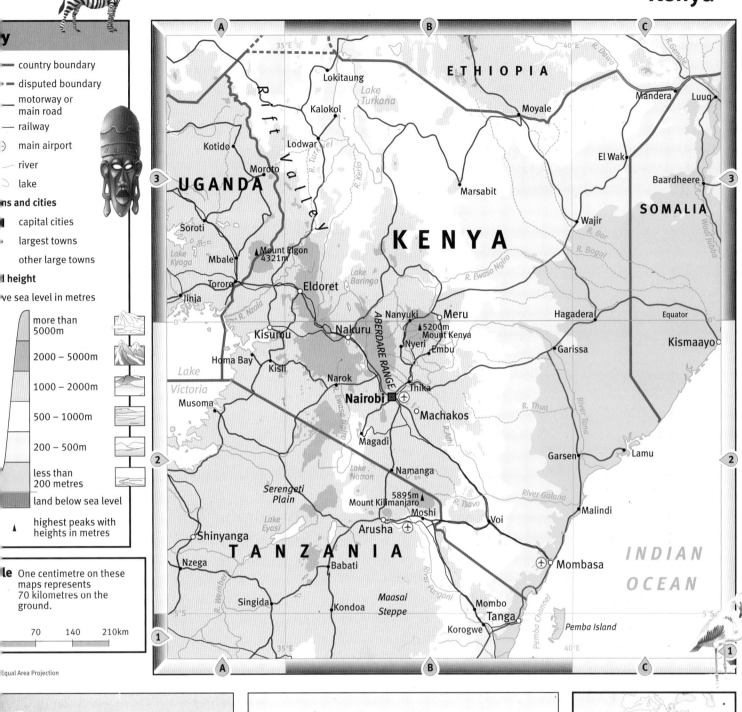

Key

- ━━━ country boundary
- ━ ━ disputed boundary
- ━━ motorway or main road
- ── railway
- ⊙ main airport
- ── river
- ⊙ lake

...ns and cities
- ■ capital cities
- ● largest towns
- ○ other large towns

...l height
...ve sea level in metres

- more than 5000m
- 2000 – 5000m
- 1000 – 2000m
- 500 – 1000m
- 200 – 500m
- less than 200 metres
- land below sea level
- ▲ highest peaks with heights in metres

...le One centimetre on these maps represents 70 kilometres on the ground.

70   140   210km

Equal Area Projection

Map labels

ETHIOPIA
Lokitaung
Lake Turkana
Kalokol
Moyale
Mandera
Luuq
Lodwar
Kotido
El Wak
Moroto
Baardheere
UGANDA
SOMALIA
Soroti
Marsabit
Wajir
Mbale
Mount Elgon 4321m
KENYA
Torora
Eldoret
Lake Baringo
R. Ewaso Ngiro
Hagadera
Equator
Jinja
Nanyuki
Meru
Kisumu
Nakuru
ABERDARE RANGE
Mount Kenya 5200m
Garissa
Kismaayo
Homa Bay
Kisii
Nyeri
Embu
Lake Victoria
Narok
Thika
Musoma
Nairobi
Machakos
R. Thua
River Tana
Magadi
Garsen
Lamu
Lake Natron
Namanga
Serengeti Plain
Mount Kilimanjaro 5895m
Moshi
Voi
Malindi
Lake Eyasi
Arusha
Shinyanga
River Galana
TANZANIA
Nzega
Babati
Mombasa
INDIAN OCEAN
Singida
Kondoa
Maasai Steppe
Mombo
Tanga
Pemba Island
Korogwe
Pemba Channel

The Maasai people herd cattle in central Kenya

Kilimanjaro is Africa's highest mountain

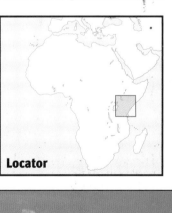

From Mombasa to Nairobi by road takes about 8 hours

Locator

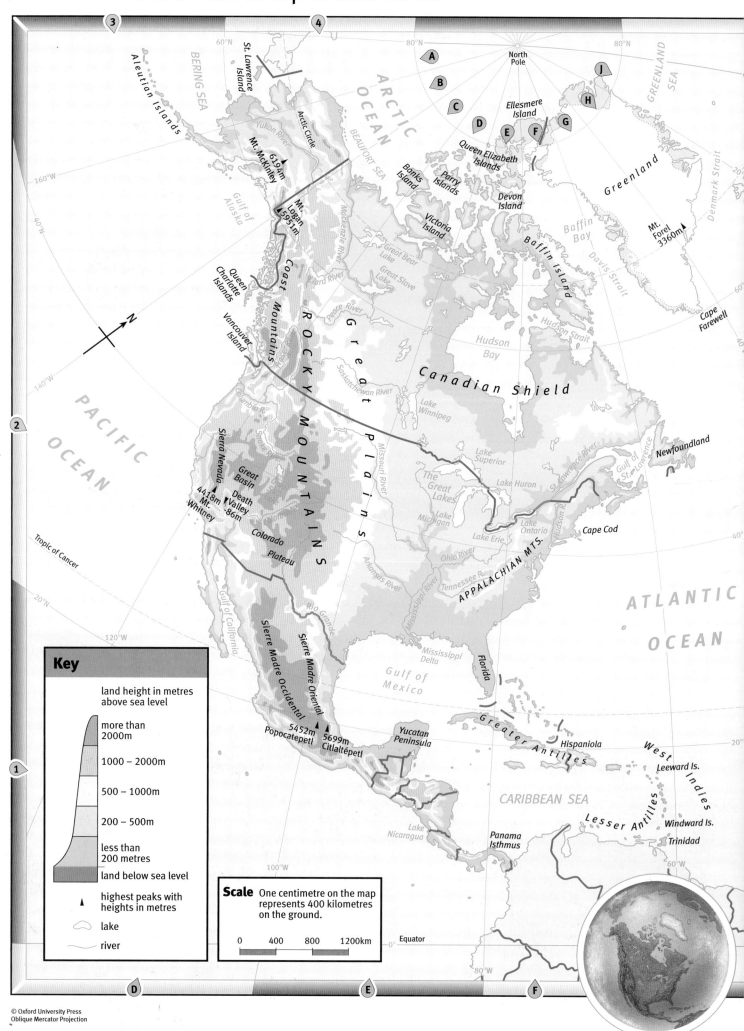

Key

land height in metres above sea level

more than 2000m

1000 – 2000m

500 – 1000m

200 – 500m

less than 200 metres

land below sea level

▲ highest peaks with heights in metres

lake

river

Scale One centimetre on the map represents 400 kilometres on the ground.

0   400   800   1200km

© Oxford University Press
Oblique Mercator Projection

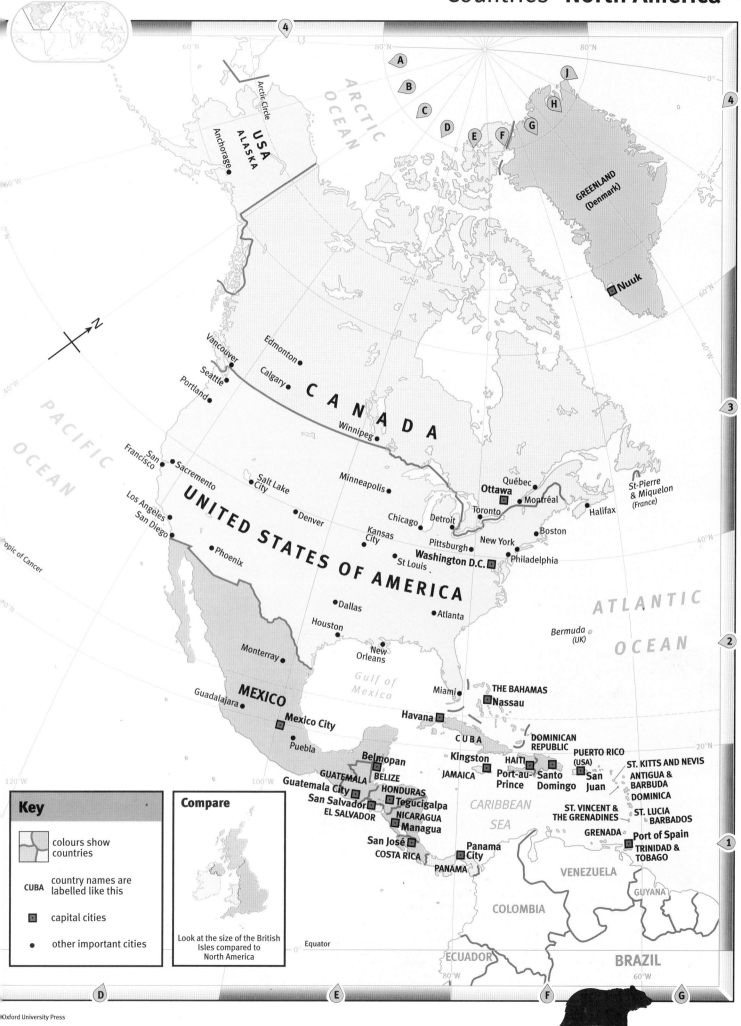

60°N 80°N 80°N 0°

A
B
C
D E F
G
H
J

ARCTIC OCEAN

Arctic Circle

USA
ALASKA
Anchorage

GREENLAND
(Denmark)

20°N

Nuuk

60°N

40°W

PACIFIC OCEAN

C A N A D A

Vancouver
Seattle
Portland
San Francisco
Sacramento
Los Angeles
San Diego

Edmonton
Calgary

Winnipeg

Salt Lake City
Denver

Minneapolis

Kansas City

Chicago
Detroit
St Louis

Québec
Ottawa
Montréal
Toronto
Pittsburgh
New York
Washington D.C.
Philadelphia
Boston
Halifax

St-Pierre & Miquelon
(France)

40°N

UNITED STATES OF AMERICA

Phoenix

Dallas

Atlanta

ATLANTIC OCEAN

Tropic of Cancer

Houston

New Orleans

Monterray

Bermuda
(UK)

2

MEXICO
Guadalajara
Mexico City
Puebla

Gulf of Mexico

Miami

Havana

CUBA

THE BAHAMAS
Nassau

Belmopan
GUATEMALA
Guatemala City
San Salvador
EL SALVADOR

BELIZE
HONDURAS
Tegucigalpa
NICARAGUA
Managua
San José
COSTA RICA
PANAMA

Kingston
JAMAICA

DOMINICAN REPUBLIC
HAITI
Port-au-Prince
Santo Domingo

PUERTO RICO
(USA)
San Juan

ST. KITTS AND NEVIS
ANTIGUA & BARBUDA
DOMINICA

CARIBBEAN SEA

ST. VINCENT & THE GRENADINES
GRENADA

ST. LUCIA
BARBADOS

20°N

Panama City
PANAMA

Port of Spain
TRINIDAD & TOBAGO

1

VENEZUELA
GUYANA
COLOMBIA

Equator

ECUADOR

BRAZIL

80°W 60°W

120°W 100°W

Key

colours show countries

CUBA country names are labelled like this

capital cities

other important cities

Compare

Look at the size of the British Isles compared to North America

Oxford University Press

D E F G

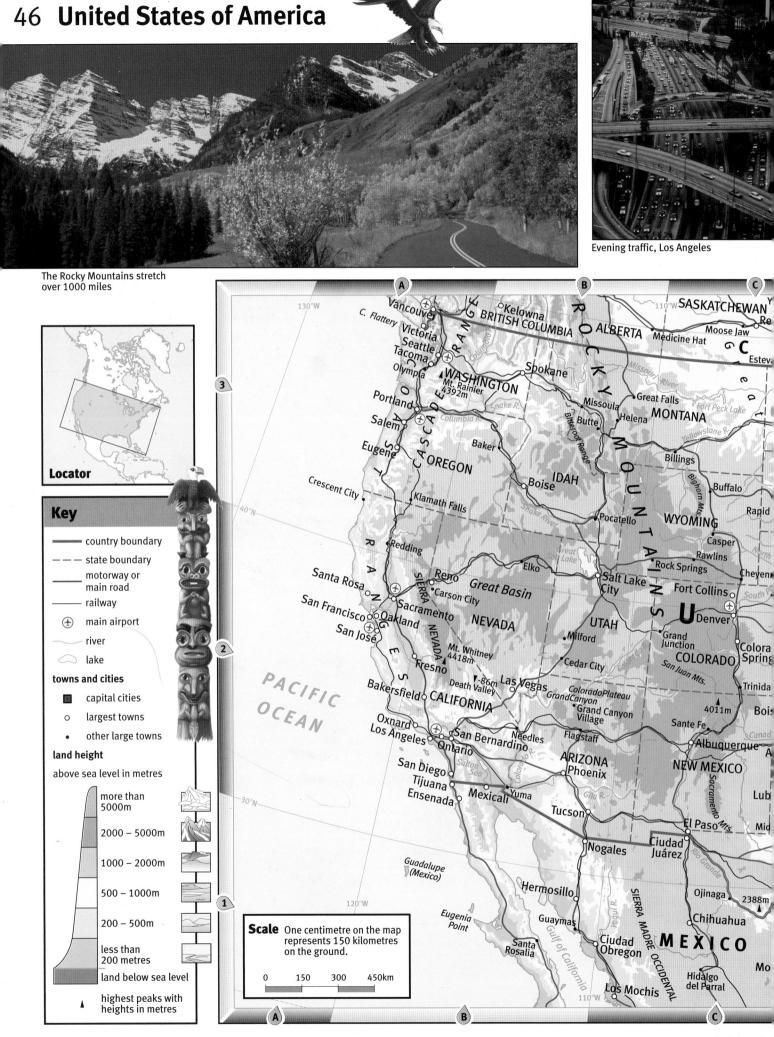

The Rocky Mountains stretch over 1000 miles

Evening traffic, Los Angeles

Locator

Key

— country boundary
-- state boundary
— motorway or main road
— railway
⊕ main airport
～ river
◠ lake

towns and cities

▪ capital cities
○ largest towns
• other large towns

land height

above sea level in metres

more than 5000m
2000 – 5000m
1000 – 2000m
500 – 1000m
200 – 500m
less than 200 metres
land below sea level
▲ highest peaks with heights in metres

Scale One centimetre on the map represents 150 kilometres on the ground.

0   150   300   450km

PACIFIC OCEAN

Vancouver
C. Flattery
Victoria
Seattle
Tacoma
Olympia
Portland
Salem
Eugene
Crescent City
Klamath Falls
Redding
Santa Rosa
San Francisco
Oakland
San José
Fresno
Bakersfield
Oxnard
Los Angeles
Ontario
San Diego
Tijuana
Ensenada

WASHINGTON
Mt. Rainier 4392m
Spokane
CASCADE RANGE
COAST RANGE
OREGON
Baker
Boise
Reno
Carson City
Sacramento
SIERRA NEVADA
Mt. Whitney 4418m
CALIFORNIA
Death Valley -86m
San Bernardino
Needles
Salton Sea
Mexicali
Yuma

BRITISH COLUMBIA
Kelowna
ALBERTA
Medicine Hat
ROCKY
Missoula
Great Falls
Helena
Butte
Bitteroot Range
MONTANA
Billings
IDAH
Pocatello
Snake R.
Snake River
Columbia R.
Great Salt Lake
Elko
Salt Lake City
NEVADA
Great Basin
Milford
UTAH
Cedar City
Las Vegas
Colorado Plateau
Grand Canyon
Grand Canyon Village
Flagstaff
ARIZONA
Phoenix
Tucson
Nogales

SASKATCHEWAN
Moose Jaw
Estev
Great
Fort Peck Lake
Yellowstone R.
Missouri River
Bighorn Mts.
Buffalo
Rapid
WYOMING
Casper
Rawlins
Rock Springs
Cheyen
Fort Collins
MOUNTAINS
U Denver
Grand Junction
COLORADO
Colora Spring
San Juan Mts.
Trinida
4011m
Sante Fe
Albuquerque
NEW MEXICO
Sacramento Mts.
El Paso
Ciudad Juárez
Rio Grande
Lub
Mid
Bois
Canad

Guadalupe (Mexico)
Eugenia Point
Hermosillo
Guaymas
Santa Rosalia
Gulf of California
Ciudad Obregon
Los Mochis
SIERRA MADRE OCCIDENTAL
Ojinaga 2388m
Chihuahua
MEXICO
Hidalgo del Parral
Mo
Yaqui R.
Gila R.
Colorado R.

130°W 110°W 120°W 110°W
40°N 30°N

...oming has fewer people than ...y other state in the USA

Manhattan skyline, New York City

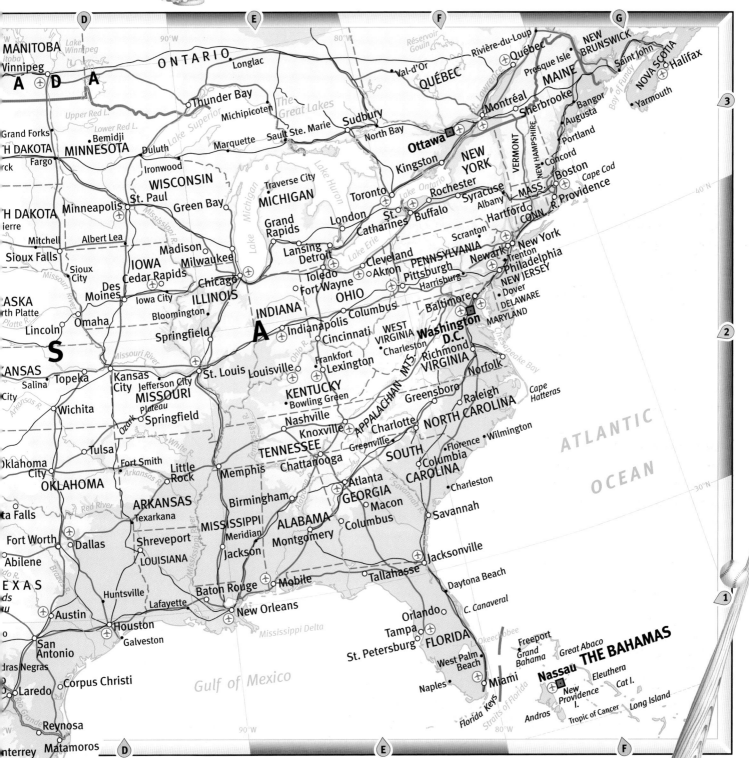

48 The Caribbean and St. Lucia

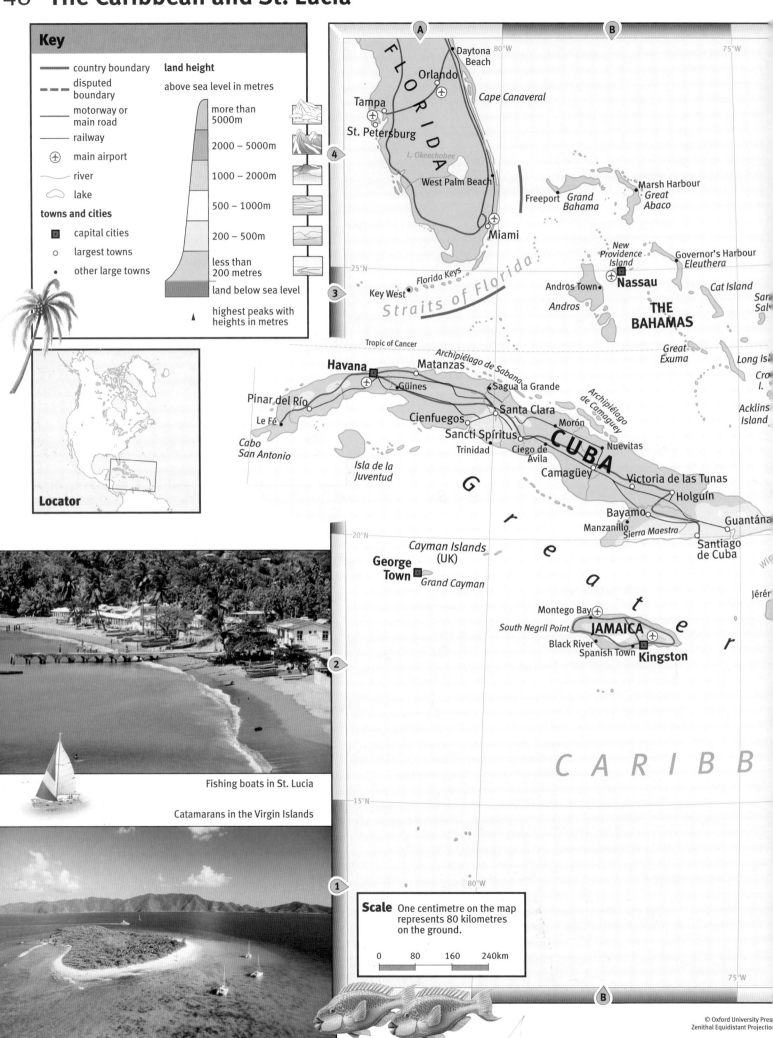

Key

———	country boundary
- - -	disputed boundary
———	motorway or main road
———	railway
⊕	main airport
∿	river
⌒	lake

towns and cities

▣	capital cities
○	largest towns
•	other large towns

land height

above sea level in metres

more than 5000m	
2000 – 5000m	
1000 – 2000m	
500 – 1000m	
200 – 500m	
less than 200 metres	
land below sea level	
▲	highest peaks with heights in metres

Locator

FLORIDA
Daytona Beach
Orlando
Cape Canaveral
Tampa
St. Petersburg
L. Okeechobee
West Palm Beach
Miami
Freeport
Grand Bahama
Marsh Harbour
Great Abaco
New Providence Island
Governor's Harbour
Eleuthera
Nassau
Andros Town
Cat Island
THE BAHAMAS
Andros
Key West
Florida Keys
Straits of Florida
Great Exuma
Long Isl
Cro I.
Acklins Island
San Sal
Tropic of Cancer

Havana
Matanzas
Güines
Archipiélago de Sabana
Pinar del Río
Sagua la Grande
Santa Clara
Le Fé
Cienfuegos
Morón
Archipiélago de Camaguey
Cabo San Antonio
Sancti Spíritus
CUBA
Nuevitas
Trinidad
Ciego de Ávila
Isla de la Juventud
Camagüey
Victoria de las Tunas
Holguín
Bayamo
Manzanillo
Sierra Maestra
Guantána
Santiago de Cuba
Jérér
Greater

Cayman Islands (UK)
George Town
Grand Cayman

Montego Bay
South Negril Point
JAMAICA
Black River
Spanish Town
Kingston

C A R I B B

Fishing boats in St. Lucia

Catamarans in the Virgin Islands

Scale One centimetre on the map represents 80 kilometres on the ground.

0   80   160   240km

St. Lucia

Saint Lucia Channel

Pte. du Cap
Pigeon Pt.
Gros Islet
Choc Bay
Monchy
Cape Marquis
Grande Rivière
Castries
Marquis
Babonneau
Grande Anse Bay
14°N
La Croix
Mairgot
La Sorcière 675m
Marigot
Anse la Raye
Grande Rivière
La Caye
Canaries
Dennery
Mt. Gimie 950m
Praslin Bay
Soufrière
Mon Repos
Micoud
Gros Piton 798m
Desruisseaux
Choiseul
Augier
Laborie
Saltibus Pt.
Vieux Fort
Cape Moule à Chique
61°W
Saint Vincent Passage

ATLANTIC OCEAN

25°N

Tropic of Cancer

20°N

Mayaguana
Caicos Passage
Caicos Islands
Grand Turk
Turks and Caicos Is. (UK)
Turks Islands

Hispaniola
Port-de-Paix
Santiago
San Francisco
DOMINICAN REPUBLIC
Cap Haïtien
La Vega
3175m
HAITI
Cordillera Central
San Pedro
Santo Domingo
Port-au-Prince
La Romana
Jacmel
Barahona
Cabo Beata

West Indies

Leeward Islands
San Juan
Charlotte Amalie
Road Town
Virgin Is. (UK)
The Valley
Anguilla (UK)
Saint Martin (Fr.)
ANTIGUA AND BARBUDA
Aguadilla
Mayagüez
Caguas
Virgin Is. (USA)
St. Maarten (Neths)
Barbuda
Codrington
La Romana
Ponce
St. Croix (USA)
St. Kitts
Antigua
St. John's
Mona Passage
Puerto Rico (USA)
Nevis
Basseterre
ST. KITTS AND NEVIS
Grande Terre
Guadeloupe (Fr.)
Plymouth
Montserrat (UK)
Pointe-á-Pitre
Marie Galente
Basse-Terre
DOMINICA
Roseau
15°N

Lesser Antilles

CARIBBEAN SEA

Martinique (Fr.)
Fort-de-France
Castries
ST. LUCIA
Vieux Fort
BARBADOS
Bridgetown
ST. VINCENT AND THE GRENADINES
St. Vincent
Kingstown
Windward Islands
St. George's
GRENADA
Tobago

Lesser Antilles
Aruba (Neths.)
Curacao (Neths.)
Bonaire (Neths.)
Punta Gallinas
Oranjestad
Willemstad
Punto Fijo
Netherlands Antilles
Isla Margarita
Port of Spain
TRINIDAD AND TOBAGO
Carúpano
Trinidad
San Fernando
Golfo de Venezuela

© Oxford University Press

CARIBBEAN SEA

ATLANTIC OCEAN

PACIFIC OCEAN

ATLANTIC OCEAN

SOUTHERN OCEAN

Cocos Islands

Galapagos Islands

Equator

Lake Maracaibo

River Orinoco

Llanos

GUIANA HIGHLANDS

Mt. Roraima 2810m

Cotopaxi 5896m
Chimborazo 6310m

River Negro

River Amazon

River Amazon

Amazon Basin

Selvas

River Tapajos

River Madeira

Rocas Island

Mato Grosso

River Tocantins

River São Francisco

BRAZILIAN HIGHLANDS

ANDES

Atacama Desert

Lake Titicaca

Lake Poopó

Tropic of Capricorn

6908m Ojos del Salado

Aconcagua 6960m

Gran Chaco

River Pilcomayo

River Paraguay

River Paraná

River Uruguay

Pampas

Rio de la Plata

Juan Fernández Islands

Colorado

R. Negro

Patagonia

Chiloé Island

Valdés Peninsula

Falkland Islands

Tierra del Fuego

Cape Horn

South Georgia

N

Key

land height in metres above sea level

more than 5000m

2000 – 5000m

1000 – 2000m

500 – 1000m

200 – 500m

less than 200 metres

land below sea level

▲ highest peaks with heights in metres

⌒ lake

∿ river

Scale One centimetre on the map represents 350 kilometres on the ground.

0   350   700   1050km

CARIBBEAN SEA

NICARAGUA

COSTA RICA

PANAMA

ATLANTIC OCEAN

Barranquilla
Maracaibo
Caracas
Valencia
VENEZUELA
Medellin
Georgetown
GUYANA SURINAME Paramaribo
Cayenne
French Guiana (France)
Cali ■ Bogota
COLOMBIA

Equator

Quito
ECUADOR
Guayaquil
Galapagos Islands (Ecuador)
Iquitos

Belem
Manaus
Rocas Island (Brazil)
Fortaleza

Trujillo
PERU
■ Lima

B R A Z I L
Recife
Salvador

Arequipa
BOLIVIA
■ La Paz
Santa Cruz
Sucre
■ Brásília
Belo Horizonte

20°S

Tropic of Capricorn

Antofagasta
PARAGUAY
■ Asunción
Rio de Janeiro
São Paulo
Curitiba
20°S

PACIFIC OCEAN

Juan Fernandez Is. (Chile)
C H I L E
Cordoba
Rosario
Porto Alegre
ATLANTIC OCEAN

Santiago ■
URUGUAY
Buenos Aires ■ Montevideo

Concepcion
ARGENTINA
Mar del Plata

N

■ Stanley
Falkland Islands (UK)

South Georgia (UK)

Punta Arenas

SOUTHERN OCEAN

Key

colours show countries

PERU country names are labelled like this

■ capital cities

• other important cities

Compare

Look at the size of the British Isles compared to South America

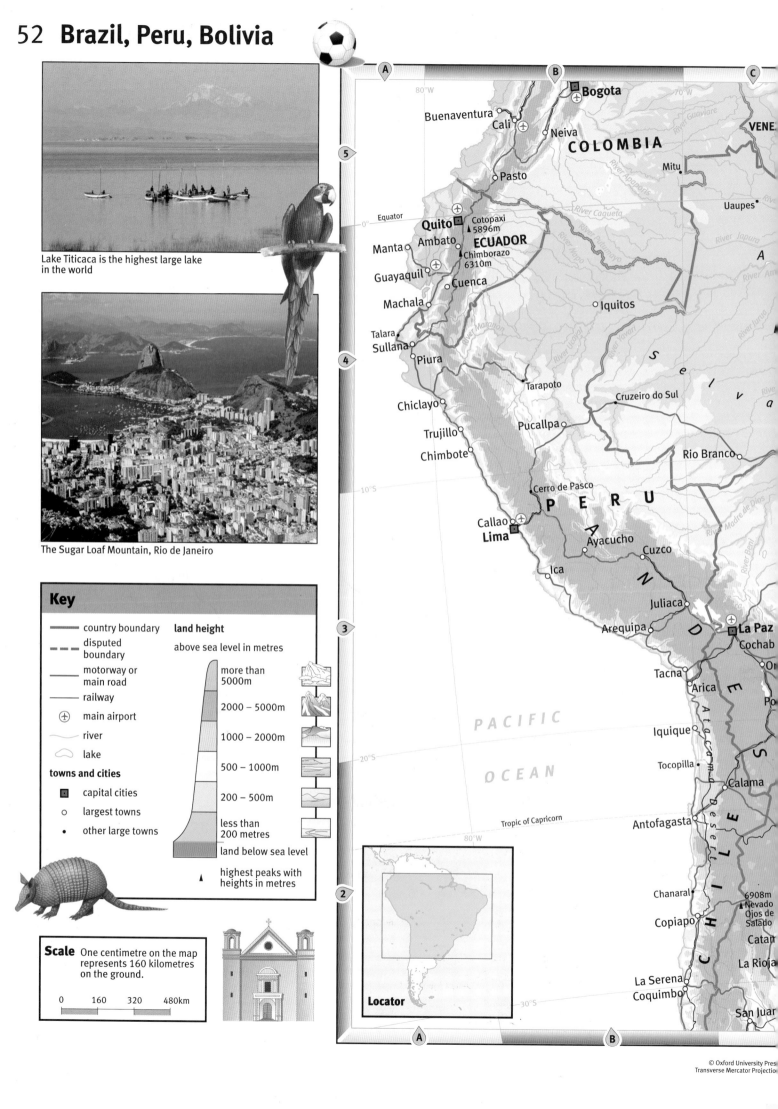

Lake Titicaca is the highest large lake in the world

The Sugar Loaf Mountain, Rio de Janeiro

Key

— country boundary

--- disputed boundary

— motorway or main road

— railway

⊕ main airport

~ river

⌒ lake

towns and cities

▣ capital cities

○ largest towns

• other large towns

land height

above sea level in metres

more than 5000m

2000 – 5000m

1000 – 2000m

500 – 1000m

200 – 500m

less than 200 metres

land below sea level

▲ highest peaks with heights in metres

Scale One centimetre on the map represents 160 kilometres on the ground.

0   160   320   480km

Locator

80°W

70°W

Bogota

Buenaventura

Cali

Neiva

COLOMBIA

VENE.

River Guaviare

Mitu

Pasto

River Apaporis

Equator 0°

Quito

Cotopaxi 5896m ▲

Manta

Ambato

ECUADOR

▲ Chimborazo 6310m

Guayaquil

Cuenca

River Caqueta

River Putumayo

River Negro

Uaupes

A

Machala

Talara

Sullana

Piura

Iquitos

River Marañon

Tarapoto

River Ucayali

River Yavari

S e l v a

River Juruá

River

Chiclayo

Pucallpa

Cruzeiro do Sul

Trujillo

Chimbote

Rio Branco

10°S

Cerro de Pasco

P E R U

River Madre de Dios

Callao

Lima

Ayacucho

A

Cuzco

River Beni

Ica

N

Juliaca

Arequipa

D

⊕ **La Paz**

Cochab

Tacna

Arica

E

On

PACIFIC

Atacama

Iquique

Po

20°S

OCEAN

Tocopila

S

Calama

Tropic of Capricorn

Antofagasta

Desert

80°W

Chanaral

6908m ▲ Nevado Ojos de Salado

Copiapo

C H I L E

Catar

La Serena

La Rioja

30°S

Coquimbo

San Juar

© Oxford University Pres

Transverse Mercator Projectio

D   E   F

60°W   50°W   40°W

GUYANA   **SURINAME**   **French Guiana (France)**

Boa Vista

Serra Tumucumaque

celos

Macapa

ATLANTIC OCEAN

5

Balbina Reservoir

Ilha de Marajo

Equator   0°

on

Manaus   Santarem   Cameta   Belem   Braganca   São Luis

Manacapuru   River Amazon   R. Xingu   Parnaiba

Coari   Itaituba   Altamira   Tucurui   Bacabal   Codo   Caxias   Sobral   Fortaleza

in   River Iriri   Maraba   Imperatriz   Teresina   Mossoro

River Madeira   River Xingu   Barra do Corda   Natal

Porto Velho   River Tapajos   Araguaina   Juazeiro do Norte   Campina Grande   Joao Pessoa

Ariquemes   River Araguaia   River Tocantins   Petrolina   Caruaru   Recife

River Teles Pires   River Parnaiba

River Arinos   Maceio

B R A Z I L   Barreiras   Diamantina   Aracaju

River Juruena   Feira de Santana   Alagoinhas

Mato Grosso   Chapada   Vitoria da Conquista   Salvador

River Guapore   Cuiaba   **BRAZILIAN**   Jequie

dad   Caceres   Rondonopolis   Anapolis   **Brasilia**   Ilheus

IVIA   Goiania   Montes Claros   River Jequitinhonha   3

Santa Cruz   Rio Verde   **HIGHLANDS**   Teofilo Otoni

Corumba   River Paranaiba   Uberlandia   Mount Itambe 2033m   Governador Valadares   Linhares

Sa. de Maracaju   Uberaba   Caratinga   Vitoria

rija   São Jose do Rio Preto   Ribeirao Preto   Belo Horizonte   Barbacena

Campo Grande   Araraquara   Juiz de Fora   Campos

Salvador   Dourados   Bauru   Nova Iguacu

ujuy   Pedro Juan Caballero   Maringa   Campinas   Santo Andre   Rio de Janeiro

Gran Chaco   **PARAGUAY**   Ponta Grossa   São Paulo   Santos

River Pilcomayo   **Asuncion**   Tropic of Capricorn

Miguel de Tucuman   River Bermejo   Formosa   Foz do Iguacu   Curitiba   Paranagua

Resistencia   Itajai   ATLANTIC OCEAN   2

GENTINA   Corrientes   Posadas   Florianopolis

Santiago del Estero   Passo Fundo

River Salado   Santa Maria   Caxias do Sul

nde   Uruguaiana   Porto Alegre

River Parana   Lagoa dos Patos

Concordia   Pelotas

Santa Fe   Parana   **URUGUAY**   Rio Grande

Cordoba   50°W   40°W   30°S

D   E   F

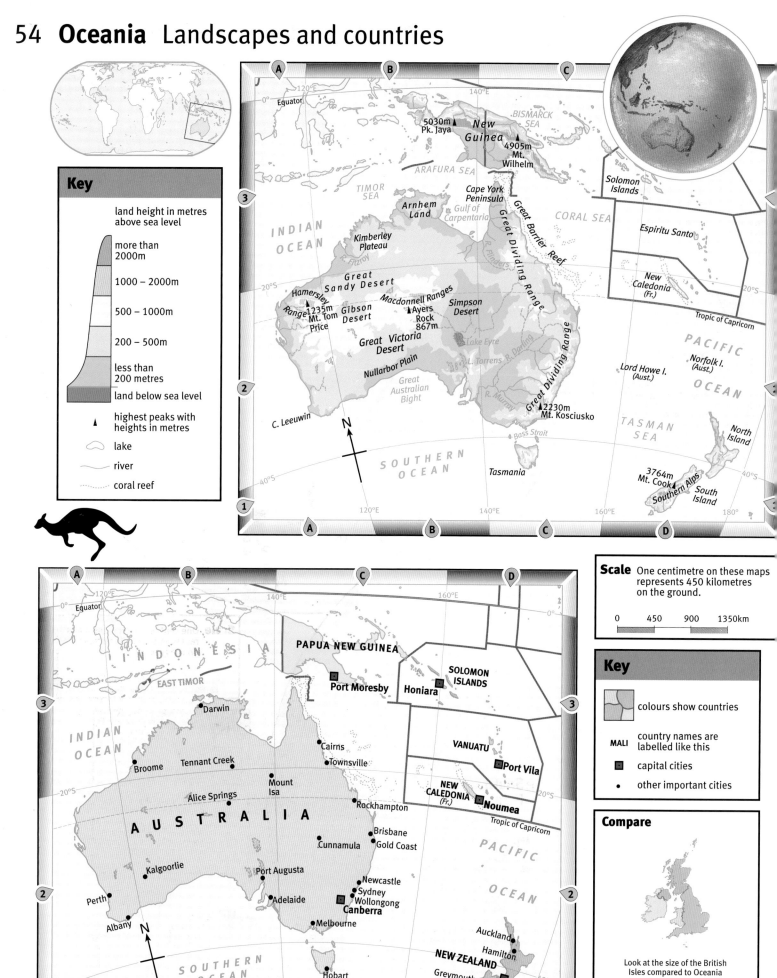

Key

land height in metres above sea level

more than 2000m

1000 – 2000m

500 – 1000m

200 – 500m

less than 200 metres

land below sea level

▲ highest peaks with heights in metres

lake

river

coral reef

Upper map labels

A   B   C

Equator   120°E   140°E

5030m Pk. Jaya   New Guinea   BISMARCK SEA

4905m Mt. Wilhelm

ARAFURA SEA   Solomon Islands

TIMOR SEA   Cape York Peninsula   CORAL SEA

Arnhem Land   Gulf of Carpentaria   Espiritu Santo

INDIAN OCEAN

Kimberley Plateau   R. Fitzroy   Great Dividing Range   New Caledonia (Fr.)

20°S   Great Sandy Desert

Hamersley Range 1235m Mt. Tom Price   Gibson Desert   Macdonnell Ranges   Ayers Rock 867m   Simpson Desert   Tropic of Capricorn

Great Victoria Desert   R. Flinders   Lake Eyre   PACIFIC

Nullarbor Plain   L. Torrens   R. Darling   Norfolk I. (Aust.)   OCEAN

C. Leeuwin   Great Australian Bight   R. Murray   Great Dividing Range   2230m Mt. Kosciusko   Lord Howe I. (Aust.)

N   Bass Strait   TASMAN SEA   North Island

40°S   SOUTHERN OCEAN   Tasmania   3764m Mt. Cook   Southern Alps   South Island

120°E   140°E   160°E   180°

A   B   C   D

Lower map labels

A   B   C   D

Equator   120°E   140°E   160°E

INDONESIA   PAPUA NEW GUINEA

EAST TIMOR   Port Moresby   SOLOMON ISLANDS   Honiara

INDIAN OCEAN   Darwin

Broome   Tennant Creek   Cairns   VANUATU   Port Vila

Townsville   20°S

Mount Isa   NEW CALEDONIA (Fr.)   Noumea

Alice Springs   Tropic of Capricorn

AUSTRALIA   Rockhampton

Kalgoorlie   Cunnamula   Brisbane   Gold Coast   PACIFIC

Port Augusta   Newcastle

Perth   Adelaide   Sydney   Wollongong   OCEAN

Albany   Canberra

N   Melbourne

SOUTHERN OCEAN   Auckland   Hamilton

Hobart   NEW ZEALAND

Greymouth   Wellington

Christchurch

40°S   Dunedin

120°E   140°E   160°E   180°

A   B   C   D

Scale

One centimetre on these maps represents 450 kilometres on the ground.

0   450   900   1350km

Key

colours show countries

MALI   country names are labelled like this

◻ capital cities

• other important cities

Compare

Look at the size of the British Isles compared to Oceania

© Oxford University Press
Zenithal Equidistant Projection

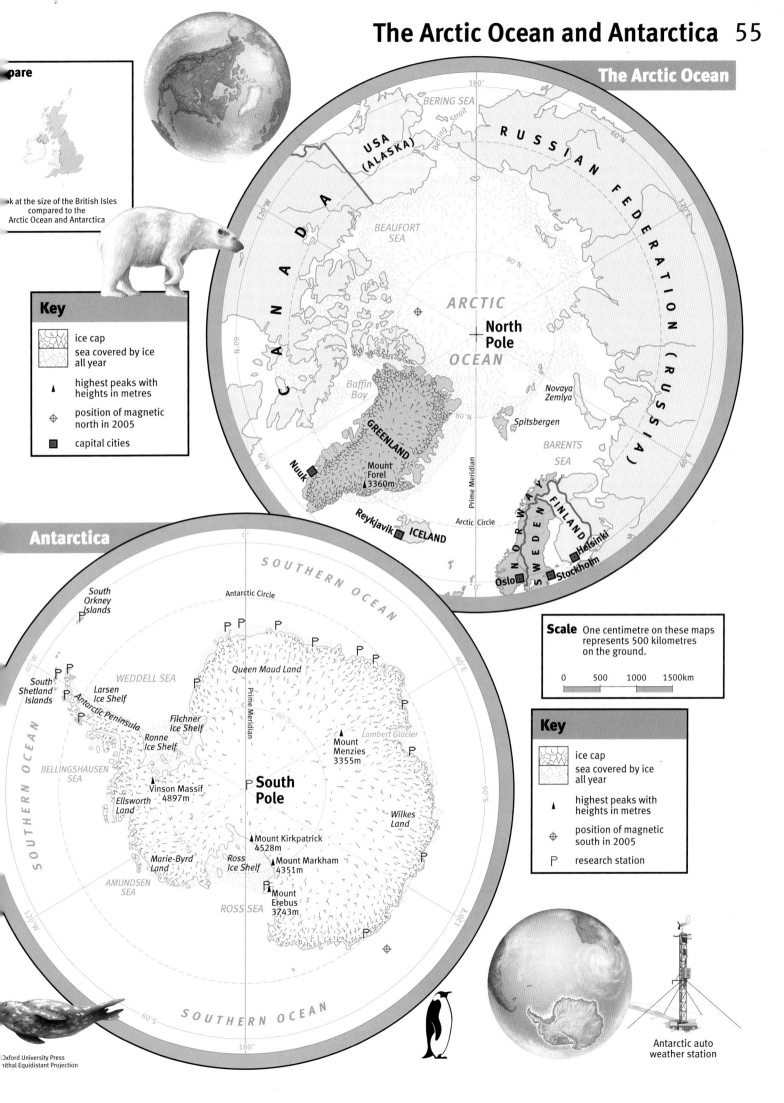

The Arctic Ocean

pare

k at the size of the British Isles
compared to the
Arctic Ocean and Antarctica

Key

- ice cap
- sea covered by ice all year
- ▲ highest peaks with heights in metres
- ⊕ position of magnetic north in 2005
- ▣ capital cities

BERING SEA
Bering Strait
USA (ALASKA)
RUSSIAN FEDERATION (RUSSIA)
60°N
120°W
120°E
BEAUFORT SEA
C A N A D A
80°N
ARCTIC
North Pole
OCEAN
80°N
Baffin Bay
Novaya Zemlya
Spitsbergen
60°N
60°E
GREENLAND
Mount Forel 3360m
BARENTS SEA
Nuuk
Prime Meridian
NORWAY
SWEDEN
FINLAND
Helsinki
Reykjavik ICELAND
Arctic Circle
Oslo
Stockholm
60°W
180°

Antarctica

South Orkney Islands
SOUTHERN OCEAN
Antarctic Circle
0°
WEDDELL SEA
Queen Maud Land
South Shetland Islands
Larsen Ice Shelf
Antarctic Peninsula
Filchner Ice Shelf
Ronne Ice Shelf
Lambert Glacier
Mount Menzies 3355m
60°W
60°E
SOUTHERN OCEAN
BELLINGSHAUSEN SEA
Vinson Massif 4897m
Prime Meridian
80°S
South Pole
Ellsworth Land
Wilkes Land
Marie-Byrd Land
Mount Kirkpatrick 4528m
Ross Ice Shelf
Mount Markham 4351m
AMUNDSEN SEA
Mount Erebus 3743m
ROSS SEA
120°W
120°E
60°S
60°S
180°
SOUTHERN OCEAN

Scale
One centimetre on these maps represents 500 kilometres on the ground.

0 500 1000 1500km

Key

- ice cap
- sea covered by ice all year
- ▲ highest peaks with heights in metres
- ⊕ position of magnetic south in 2005
- P research station

Antarctic auto weather station

Oxford University Press
nithal Equidistant Projection

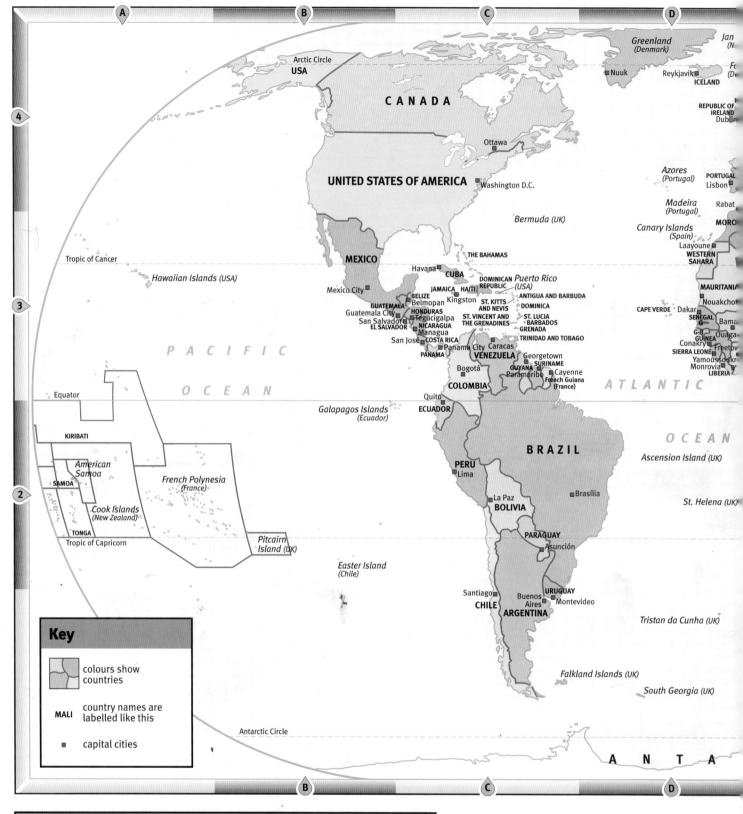

A   B   C   D

Greenland
(Denmark)

Jan
(N:

Arctic Circle
USA

Nuuk

Reykjavík
ICELAND

Fo
(De

REPUBLIC OF
IRELAND
Dublir

C A N A D A

Ottawa

4

UNITED STATES OF AMERICA

Washington D.C.

Azores
(Portugal)

PORTUGAL
Lisbon

Bermuda (UK)

Madeira
(Portugal)

Rabat

Tropic of Cancer

Hawaiian Islands (USA)

MEXICO

Havana

Mexico City

THE BAHAMAS

CUBA

Canary Islands
(Spain)

Laayoune
**WESTERN
SAHARA**

MORO

3

**DOMINICAN
REPUBLIC**

Puerto Rico
(USA)

MAURITANIA

Nouakchot

JAMAICA **HAITI**

BELIZE

Kingston

GUATEMALA Belmopan

HONDURAS

ANTIGUA AND BARBUDA

**ST. KITTS
AND NEVIS**

DOMINICA

CAPE VERDE Dakar
SENEGAL

Bama

Guatemala City

Tegucigalpa

San Salvador **NICARAGUA**

EL SALVADOR

Managua

**ST. VINCENT AND
THE GRENADINES**

ST. LUCIA
BARBADOS
GRENADA

G-B

GUINEA Ouaga

Conakry

Freetoy

P A C I F I C

San José **COSTA RICA**

PANAMA

Panama City

Caracas

TRINIDAD AND TOBAGO

SIERRA LEONE

Yamoussouki

Monrovia

LIBERIA

VENEZUELA

Georgetown

SURINAME

Bogotá

GUYANA

Paramaribo Cayenne

O C E A N

COLOMBIA

French Guiana
(France)

A T L A N T I C

Equator

Quito

Galapagos Islands
(Ecuador)

ECUADOR

O C E A N

KIRIBATI

B R A Z I L

Ascension Island (UK)

American
Samoa

French Polynesia
(France)

PERU

Lima

SAMOA

La Paz

Brasília

St. Helena (UK)

Cook Islands
(New Zealand)

BOLIVIA

2

TONGA

Tropic of Capricorn

Pitcairn
Island (UK)

PARAGUAY

Asunción

Easter Island
(Chile)

Santiago

Buenos
Aires

URUGUAY

Montevideo

Tristan da Cunha (UK)

CHILE

ARGENTINA

Key

colours show
countries

MALI

country names are
labelled like this

capital cities

Falkland Islands (UK)

South Georgia (UK)

Antarctic Circle

A N T A

B   C   D

Abbreviations

A	ALBANIA	G	THE GAMBIA	R	ROMANIA
AR	ARMENIA	G-B	GUINEA-BISSAU	S	SLOVAKIA
AU	AUSTRIA	H	HUNGARY	SE	SERBIA
AZ	AZERBAIJAN	IS	ISRAEL	SL	SLOVENIA
B	BELGIUM	L	LEBANON	SW	SWITZERLAND
BE	BENIN	LI	LITHUANIA	T	TAJIKISTAN
BH	BOSNIA-HERZEGOVINA	LU	LUXEMBOURG	TU	TURKMENISTAN
BR	BRUNEI	M	FORMER YUGOSLAV	U	UGANDA
BU	BURKINA		REPUBLIC OF MACEDONIA	UAE	UNITED ARAB EMIRATES
C	CROATIA	MT	MONTENEGRO	ZIM	ZIMBABWE
CAR	CENTRAL AFRICAN REPUBLIC	N	NETHERLANDS		
CZ	CZECH REPUBLIC	Q	QATAR		

North America

South America

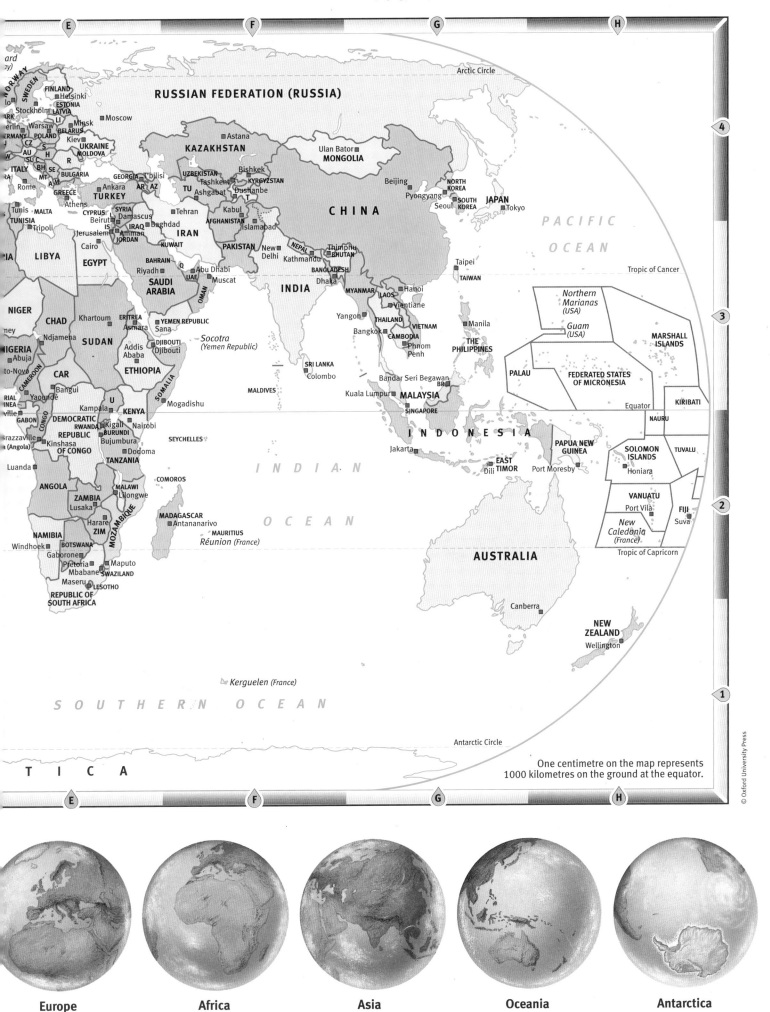

RUSSIAN FEDERATION (RUSSIA)

NORWAY SWEDEN FINLAND Helsinki
Stockholm ESTONIA Moscow
Warsaw LATVIA
POLAND BELARUS Minsk
Kiev UKRAINE Astana
MOLDOVA KAZAKHSTAN
Ulan Bator MONGOLIA
ITALY BULGARIA GEORGIA Tbilisi UZBEKISTAN Bishkek
Rome GREECE TURKEY AR AZ Tashkent KYRGYZSTAN Beijing
Athens Ankara Ashgabat Dushanbe NORTH KOREA
TUNISIA MALTA CYPRUS SYRIA Damascus TU Kabul Pyongyang
Tripoli Beirut IRAQ Baghdad IRAN AFGHANISTAN CHINA SOUTH Seoul JAPAN Tokyo
Jerusalem Amman Tehran Islamabad KOREA
Cairo JORDAN KUWAIT PAKISTAN New Delhi NEPAL Thimphu Taipei
LIBYA EGYPT BAHRAIN Riyadh Abu Dhabi Kathmandu BHUTAN TAIWAN
NIGER SAUDI ARABIA UAE OMAN Muscat INDIA BANGLADESH Dhaka
CHAD Khartoum ERITREA YEMEN REPUBLIC MYANMAR LAOS Hanoi
NIGERIA Abuja SUDAN Asmara Sana Yangon THAILAND Vientiane Manila
Ndjamena Addis DJIBOUTI Socotra Bangkok VIETNAM MARSHALL ISLANDS
CAR Ababa Djibouti CAMBODIA Phnom THE PHILIPPINES
Yaoundé ETHIOPIA SRI LANKA Penh Northern Marianas (USA)
GABON CONGO U KENYA Colombo MALDIVES Kuala Lumpur Guam (USA)
Kampala Mogadishu Bandar Seri Begawan PALAU FEDERATED STATES OF MICRONESIA
DEMOCRATIC RWANDA Kigali Nairobi SINGAPORE MALAYSIA KIRIBATI
REPUBLIC BURUNDI Bujumbura SEYCHELLES Equator NAURU
OF CONGO Dodoma INDONESIA PAPUA NEW GUINEA SOLOMON ISLANDS TUVALU
Luanda TANZANIA Jakarta EAST Honiara
ANGOLA COMOROS TIMOR Port Moresby
ZAMBIA MALAWI Dili VANUATU FIJI
Lusaka Lilongwe MADAGASCAR Port Vila Suva
NAMIBIA ZIM Harare Antananarivo MAURITIUS New Caledonia (France)
Windhoek BOTSWANA MOZAMBIQUE Réunion (France) AUSTRALIA
Gaborone Maputo
Pretoria Mbabane SWAZILAND Canberra
Maseru LESOTHO NEW ZEALAND
REPUBLIC OF SOUTH AFRICA Wellington

Kerguelen (France)

SOUTHERN OCEAN

ANTARCTICA

PACIFIC OCEAN
INDIAN OCEAN
Arctic Circle
Tropic of Cancer
Equator
Tropic of Capricorn
Antarctic Circle

One centimetre on the map represents 1000 kilometres on the ground at the equator.

© Oxford University Press

Europe **Africa** **Asia** **Oceania** **Antarctica**

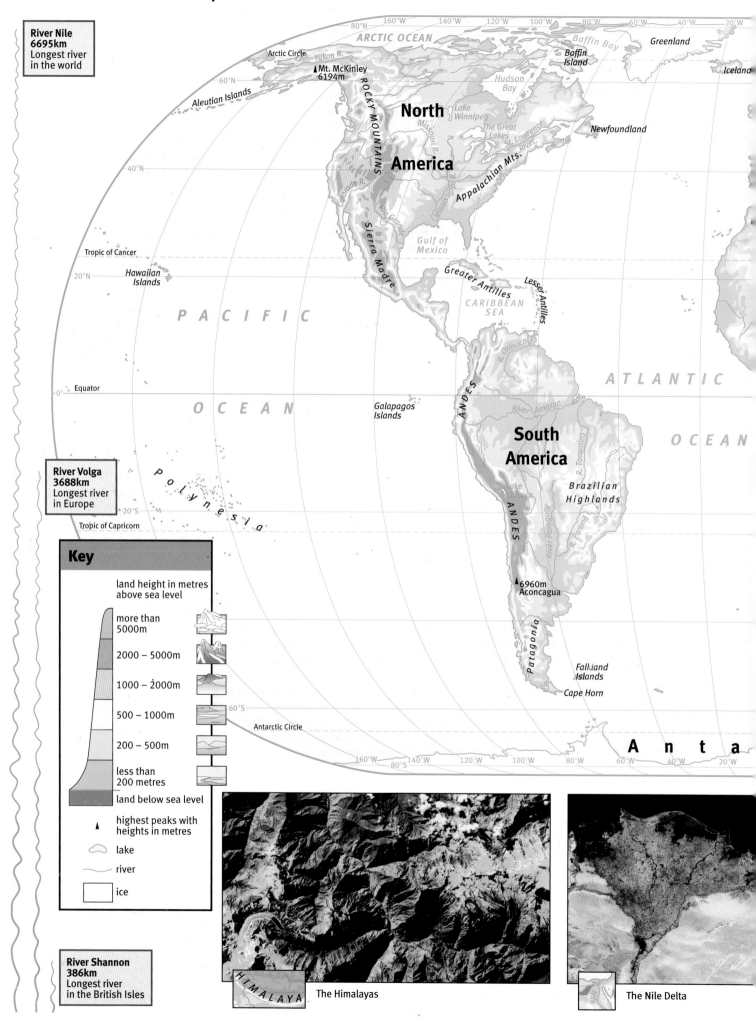

River Nile
6695km
Longest river
in the world

ARCTIC OCEAN

Arctic Circle

Yukon R.

Mt. McKinley
6194m

Aleutian Islands

ROCKY MOUNTAINS

North

America

Greenland

Baffin Bay

Baffin
Island

Iceland

Hudson
Bay

Lake
Winnipeg

Missouri R.

The Great
Lakes

St. Lawrence River

Newfoundland

Appalachian Mts.

Mississippi

Colorado R.

Rio Grande

Sierra Madre

Gulf of
Mexico

Greater Antilles

Lesser Antilles

CARIBBEAN
SEA

Tropic of Cancer

Hawaiian
Islands

PACIFIC

OCEAN

Galapagos
Islands

R. Orinoco

River Amazon

ATLANTIC

OCEAN

Equator

Polynesia

River Volga
3688km
Longest river
in Europe

ANDES

South
America

Brazilian
Highlands

R. Tocantins

Tropic of Capricorn

Lake
Titicaca

ANDES

River Paraguay

R. Paraná

6960m
Aconcagua

Key

land height in metres
above sea level

Patagonia

more than
5000m

2000 – 5000m

1000 – 2000m

Falkland
Islands

500 – 1000m

Cape Horn

200 – 500m

Antarctic Circle

less than
200 metres

land below sea level

▲ highest peaks with
heights in metres

⬭ lake

〰 river

☐ ice

A n t a

River Shannon
386km
Longest river
in the British Isles

HIMALAYA

The Himalayas

Nile

The Nile Delta

© Oxford University Pr
Eckert IV Project

ARCTIC OCEAN

Arctic Circle

andinavia
Lake Ladoga

URAL MOUNTAINS

River Volga

River Ob'

Yenisey River

R. Lena

SEA OF OKHOTSK

BERING SEA

60°N

S i b e r i a

Lake Baykal

R. Amur

Europe
lanc
River Danube
LPS

BLACK SEA

CAUCASUS

TAURUS MTS.

ZAGROS MTS.

CASPIAN SEA

ARAL SEA

River Irtysh

Lake Balkhash

ALTAI MOUNTAINS

Gobi Desert

Asia

8611m
▲K2

Plateau of Tibet

40°N

Honshu

Huang He

EAST CHINA SEA

MEDITERRANEAN SEA

Qattara
Depression
-133m ▲

Arabian
Peninsula

RED SEA

The Gulf

R. Indus

H I M A L A Y A

Mt. Everest
8848m ▲

R. Ganges

Deccan

Irrawaddy R.

Chong Jiang

Tropic of Cancer

20°N

ara

Lake Chad

Blue Nile

Blue Nile R.

ARABIAN SEA

Bay of Bengal

Mekong R.

SOUTH CHINA SEA

P A C I F I C

M i c r o n e s i a

Africa

River Congo

Lake Victoria

5895m
▲ Kilimanjaro

I N D I A N

4094m
▲Kinabalu

Borneo

O C E A N

M e l a n e s i a

Equator

Lake Tanganyika

Lake Nyasa

R. Zambezi

Sumatra

5030m
Jaya Peak ▲

New Guinea

O C E A N

Madagascar

Java

Oceania

CORAL SEA

Namib Desert

Limpopo R.

Kalahari Desert

Drakensberg

Macdonnell Ranges

Great Dividing Range

Tropic of Capricorn

20°S

Cape of Good Hope

R. Darling

R. Murray

TASMAN SEA

North Island

S. ALPS

40°S

South Island

Kerguelen

S O U T H E R N   O C E A N

60°S

Antarctic Circle

tica

20°E   40°E   60°E   80°E   100°E   120°E   140°E   160°E   80°S

Mount Everest
Highest mountain in the world

Mont Blanc
Highest mountain in Europe

Ben Nevis
Highest mountain in the British Isles

metres
8848
8000
7000
6000
5000
4807
4000
3000
2000
1344
1000
500

The River Mississippi and St. Louis

The Great Lakes

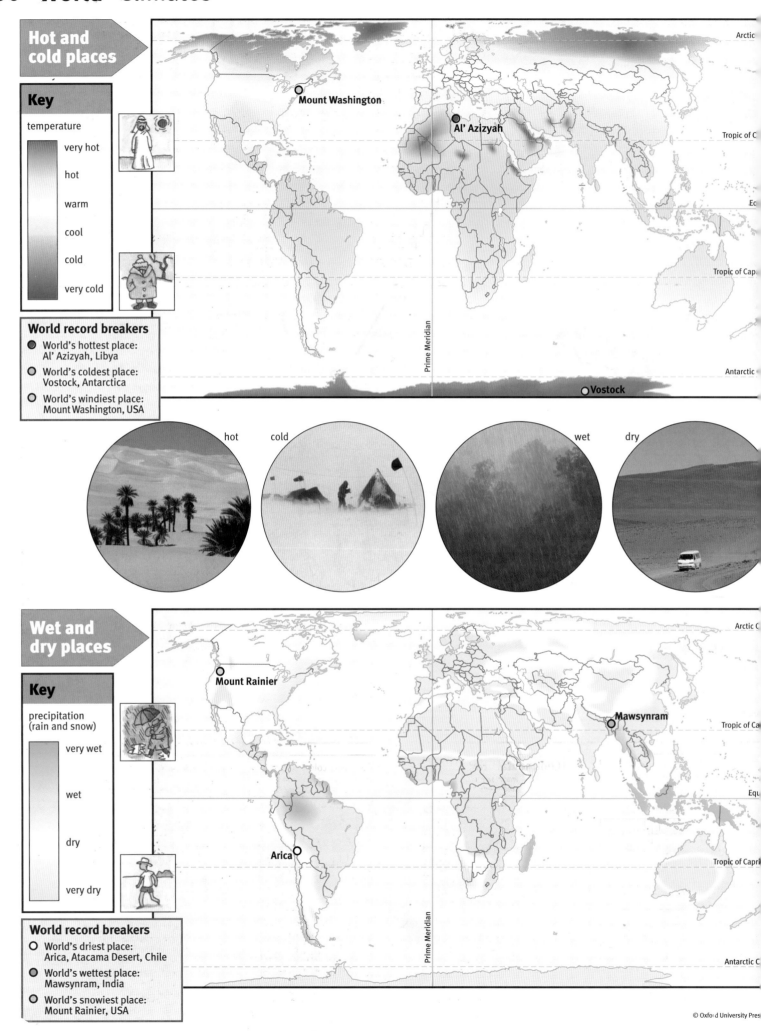

Hot and cold places

Key

temperature

very hot
hot
warm
cool
cold
very cold

World record breakers

- World's hottest place:
  Al' Azizyah, Libya
- World's coldest place:
  Vostock, Antarctica
- World's windiest place:
  Mount Washington, USA

Mount Washington

Al' Azizyah

Vostock

Arctic

Tropic of C

Ec

Tropic of Cap

Antarctic

hot   cold   wet   dry

Wet and dry places

Key

precipitation
(rain and snow)

very wet

wet

dry

very dry

World record breakers

- World's driest place:
  Arica, Atacama Desert, Chile
- World's wettest place:
  Mawsynram, India
- World's snowiest place:
  Mount Rainier, USA

Mount Rainier

Mawsynram

Arica

Arctic C

Tropic of Ca

Equ

Tropic of Capri

Antarctic C

© Oxford University Pres

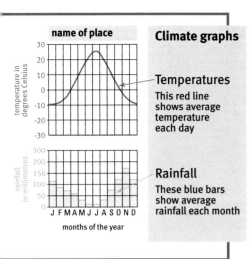

name of place

Climate graphs

Temperatures
This red line shows average temperature each day

Rainfall
These blue bars show average rainfall each month

temperature in degrees Celsius

rainfall in millimetres

months of the year

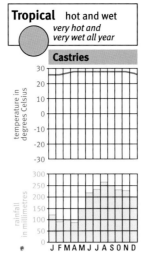

Tropical hot and wet
very hot and very wet all year

Castries

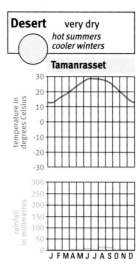

Desert very dry
hot summers cooler winters

Tamanrasset

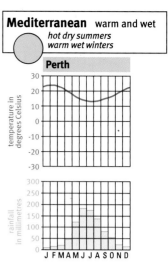

Mediterranean warm and wet
hot dry summers warm wet winters

Perth

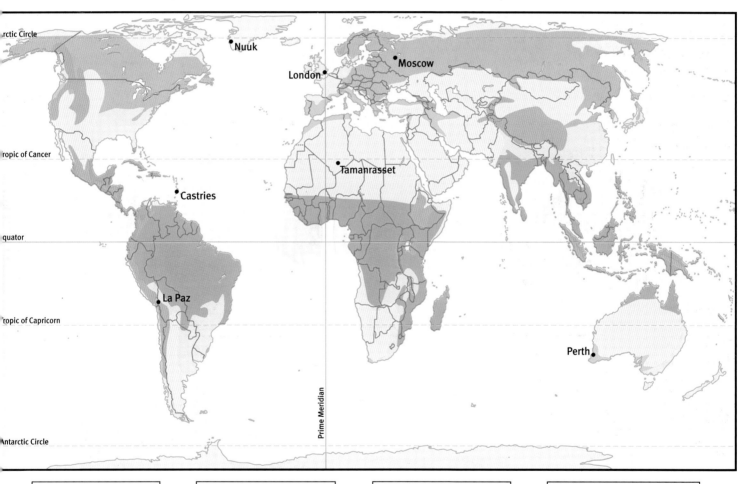

rctic Circle

Nuuk

Moscow

London

ropic of Cancer

Tamanrasset

Castries

quator

La Paz

ropic of Capricorn

Perth

Prime Meridian

ntarctic Circle

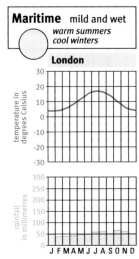

Maritime mild and wet
warm summers cool winters

London

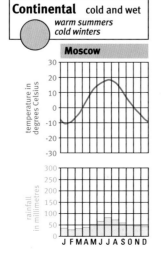

Continental cold and wet
warm summers cold winters

Moscow

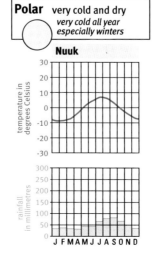

Polar very cold and dry
very cold all year especially winters

Nuuk

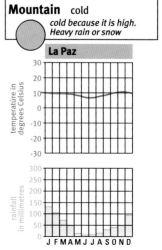

Mountain cold
cold because it is high. Heavy rain or snow

La Paz

Oxford University Press
kert IV projection

There are about 6 485 000 000 people in the world.

ARCTIC OCEAN

Arctic Circle

Chicago
New York
Washington D.C. Philadelphia
San Francisco
Los Angeles

Tropic of Cancer

Mexico City

PACIFIC
OCEAN

ATLANTIC

Bogotá

OCEAN

Equator

Lima-Callao

Tropic of Capricorn

Rio de Janeiro
São Paulo

Buenos Aires

Antarctic Circle

Key

Population density

people per square kilometre

- over 100
- 5–100
- under 5

■ cities with more than six million (6 000 000) people

— country boundary

Population pyramid

If there were just 100 people in the world, this is how old they would be:

- 80 years old and over
- between 70 and 79
- between 60 and 69
- between 50 and 59
- between 40 and 49
- between 30 and 39
- between 20 and 29
- between 10 and 19
- 9 years old and under

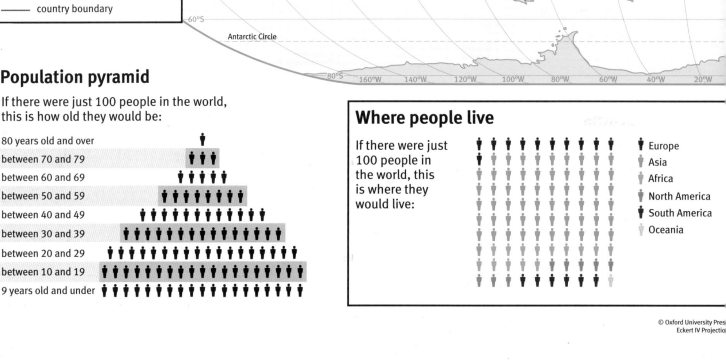

Where people live

If there were just 100 people in the world, this is where they would live:

- Europe
- Asia
- Africa
- North America
- South America
- Oceania

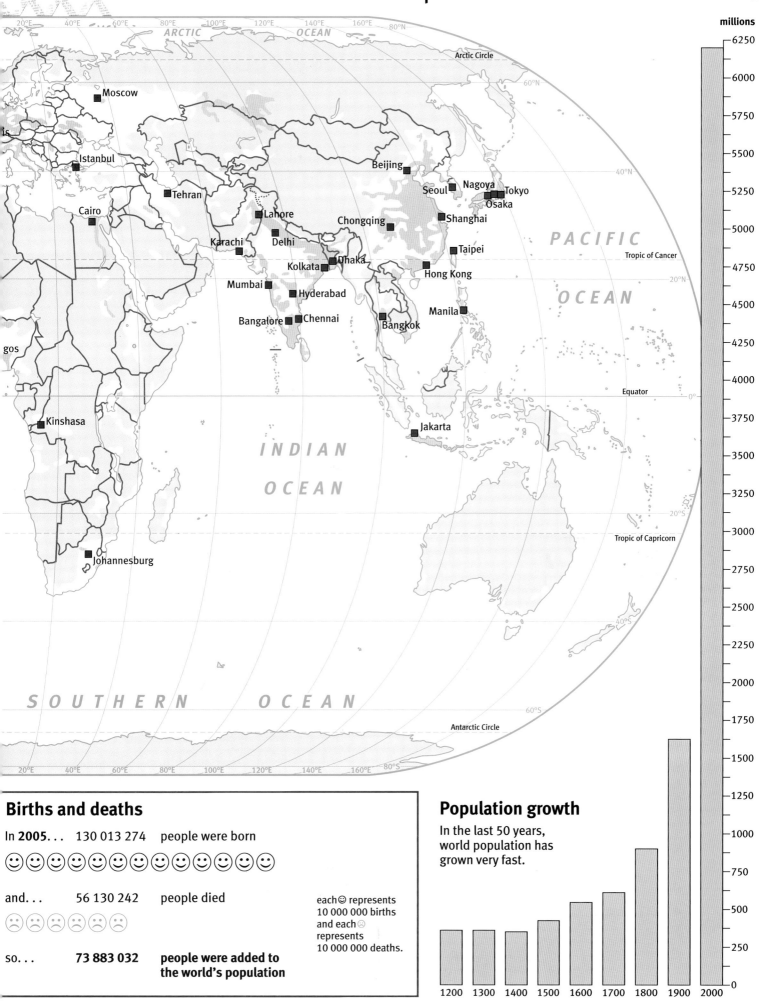

millions

ARCTIC OCEAN

Arctic Circle

60°N

Moscow

40°N

Istanbul

Beijing

Seoul Nagoya Tokyo

Osaka

Tehran

Shanghai

PACIFIC

Cairo

Lahore

Chongqing

Tropic of Cancer

Karachi Delhi

Taipei

20°N

OCEAN

Dhaka

Kolkata

Hong Kong

Mumbai Hyderabad

Manila

Bangalore Chennai

Bangkok

Equator 0°

INDIAN

Jakarta

OCEAN

20°S

Tropic of Capricorn

Johannesburg

40°S

S O U T H E R N   O C E A N

60°S

Antarctic Circle

80°S

20°E   40°E   60°E   80°E   100°E   120°E   140°E   160°E

Kinshasa

Births and deaths

In **2005**. . .   130 013 274   people were born

☺ ☺ ☺ ☺ ☺ ☺ ☺ ☺ ☺ ☺ ☺ ☺ ☺

and. . .   56 130 242   people died

☹ ☹ ☹ ☹ ☹ ☹

so. . .   **73 883 032**   **people were added to the world's population**

each ☺ represents 10 000 000 births and each ☹ represents 10 000 000 deaths.

Population growth

In the last 50 years, world population has grown very fast.

1200 1300 1400 1500 1600 1700 1800 1900 2000

6250
6000
5750
5500
5250
5000
4750
4500
4250
4000
3750
3500
3250
3000
2750
2500
2250
2000
1750
1500
1250
1000
750
500
250
0

tropical forest

deciduous forest

coniferous forest

ARCTIC OCEAN

80°N

160°W   140°W   120°W   100°W   80°W   60°W   40°W   20°W

Arctic Circle

60°N

40°N

Tropic of Cancer

20°N

PACIFIC

Equator   0°

OCEAN

ATLANTIC

OCEAN

20°S

Tropic of Capricorn

40°S

60°S

Antarctic Circle

80°S

160°W   140°W   120°W   100°W   80°W   60°W   40°W   20°W

Key

	coniferous forest
	trees have leaves all year
	deciduous forest
	trees drop their leaves in winter
	tropical forest
	tall trees growing close together
	savannah
	tall trees and scattered trees
	temperate grassland
	prairies, steppes, pampas and veld
	semi desert
	short grass and small dry bushes
	desert
	sand and stones with few plants
	tundra
	moss and bog with some short trees
	ice
	no plants
	mountains
	thin soils and steep slopes

desert

semi desert

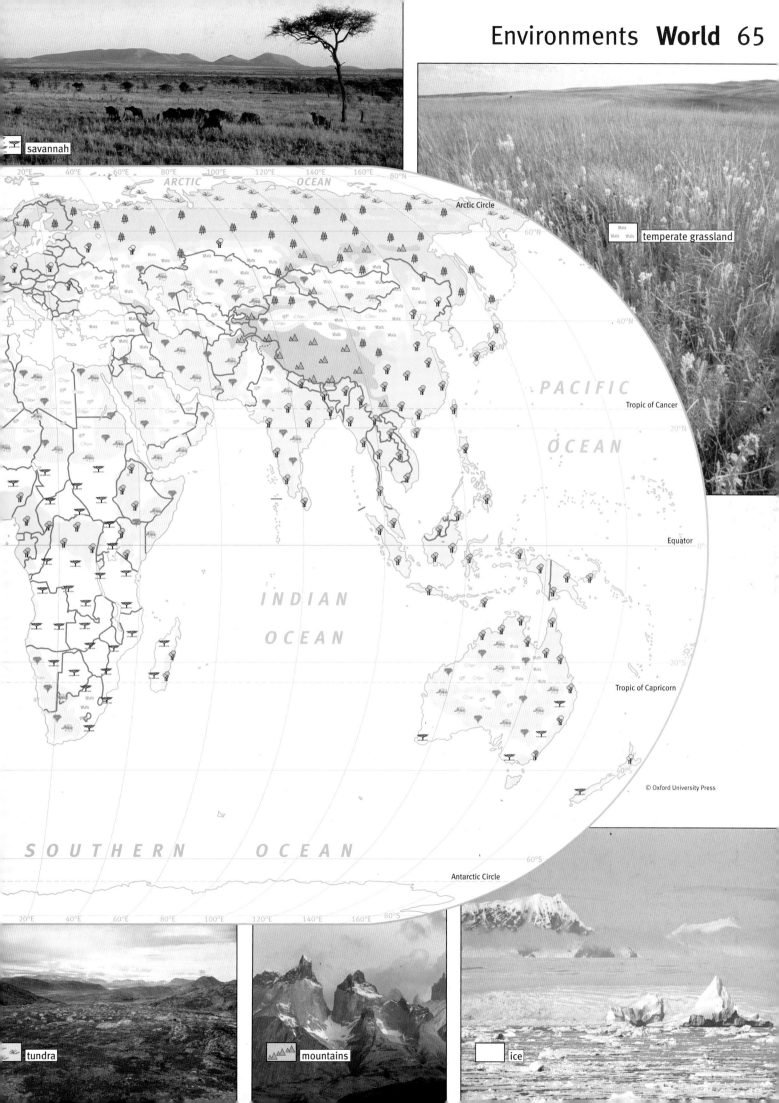

savannah

temperate grassland

ARCTIC OCEAN

Arctic Circle

60°N

40°N

PACIFIC

Tropic of Cancer

20°N

OCEAN

Equator

INDIAN

OCEAN

20°S

Tropic of Capricorn

60°S

SOUTHERN OCEAN

Antarctic Circle

80°S

© Oxford University Press

tundra

mountains

ice

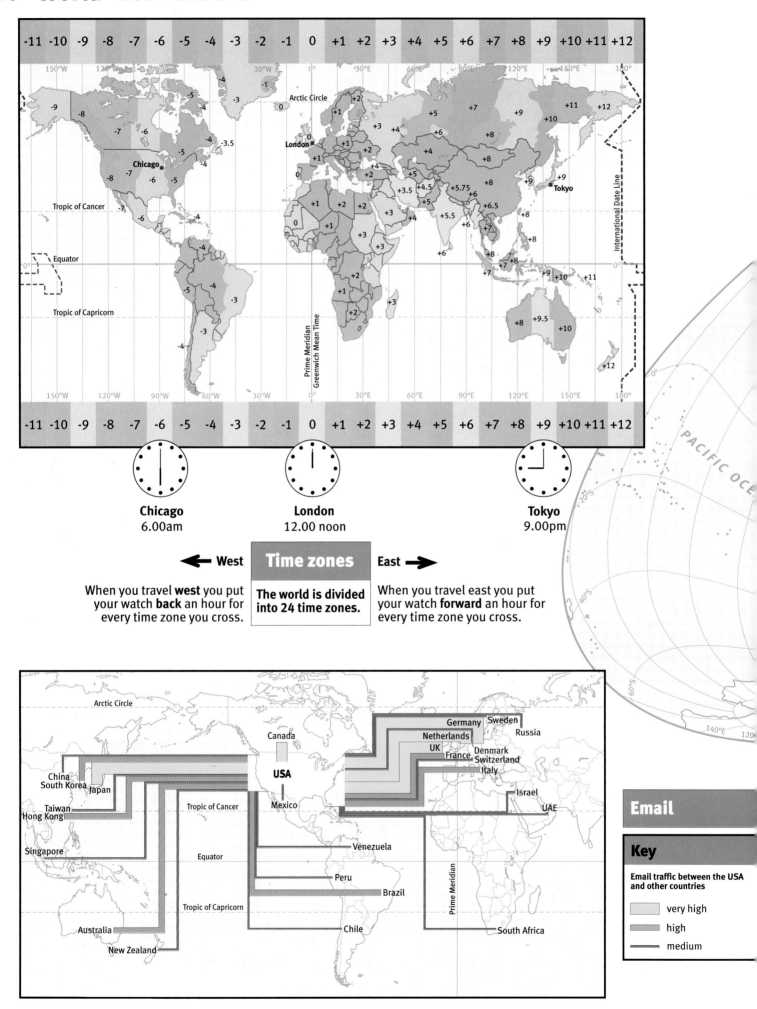

| -11 | -10 | -9 | -8 | -7 | -6 | -5 | -4 | -3 | -2 | -1 | 0 | +1 | +2 | +3 | +4 | +5 | +6 | +7 | +8 | +9 | +10 | +11 | +12 |

Chicago 6.00am

London 12.00 noon

Tokyo 9.00pm

← **West**

Time zones

East →

When you travel **west** you put your watch **back** an hour for every time zone you cross.

The world is divided into 24 time zones.

When you travel east you put your watch **forward** an hour for every time zone you cross.

Email

Key

Email traffic between the USA and other countries

very high
high

The distance round the Earth at
the Equator is 40 075 kilometres
(24 846 miles)

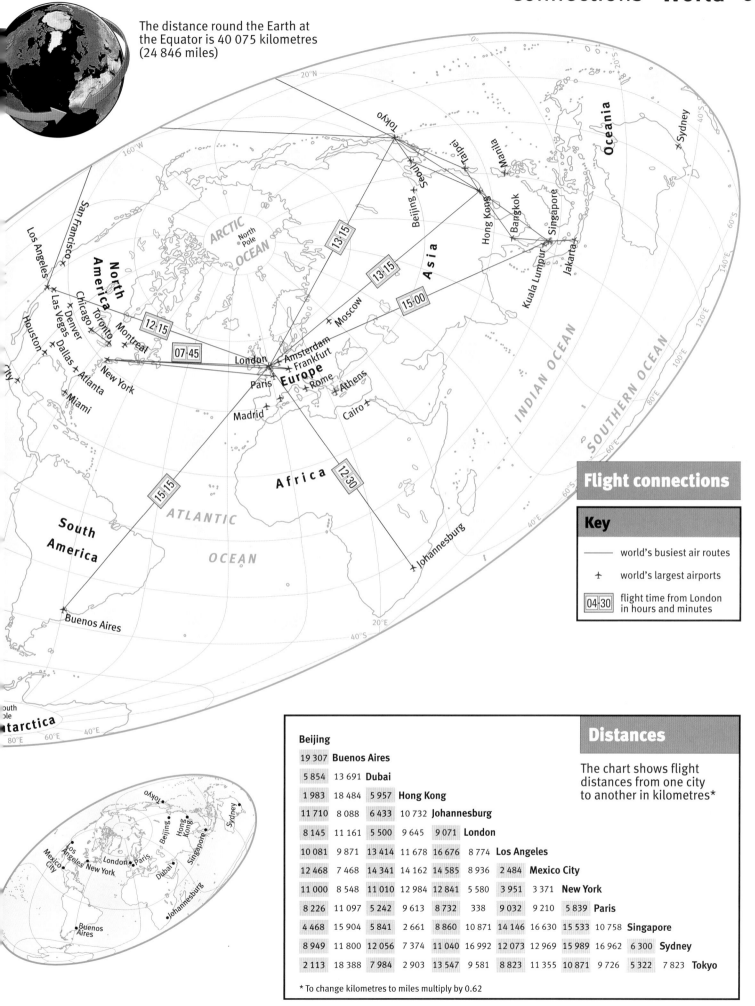

Flight connections

Key

——	world's busiest air routes
✈	world's largest airports
04·30	flight time from London in hours and minutes

Flight times shown on map: 12·15, 07·45, 13·15, 13·15, 15·00, 15·15, 12·30

Distances

The chart shows flight
distances from one city
to another in kilometres*

Beijing										
19 307	**Buenos Aires**									
5 854	13 691	**Dubai**								
1 983	18 484	5 957	**Hong Kong**							
11 710	8 088	6 433	10 732	**Johannesburg**						
8 145	11 161	5 500	9 645	9 071	**London**					
10 081	9 871	13 414	11 678	16 676	8 774	**Los Angeles**				
12 468	7 468	14 341	14 162	14 585	8 936	2 484	**Mexico City**			
11 000	8 548	11 010	12 984	12 841	5 580	3 951	3 371	**New York**		
8 226	11 097	5 242	9 613	8 732	338	9 032	9 210	5 839	**Paris**	
4 468	15 904	5 841	2 661	8 860	10 871	14 146	16 630	15 533	10 758	**Singapore**
8 949	11 800	12 056	7 374	11 040	16 992	12 073	12 969	15 989	16 962	6 300	**Sydney**
2 113	18 388	7 984	2 903	13 547	9 581	8 823	11 355	10 871	9 726	5 322	7 823	**Tokyo**

* To change kilometres to miles multiply by 0.62

Oxford University Press
...blique Aitoff Projection

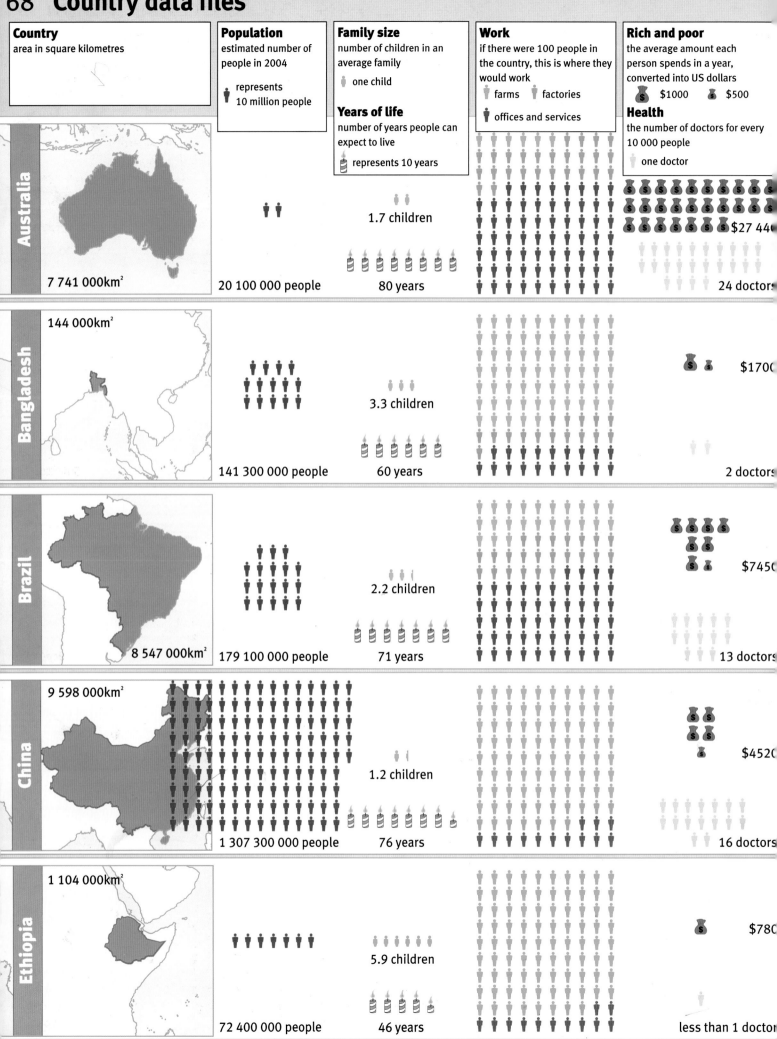

Country
area in square kilometres

Population
estimated number of people in 2004

represents 10 million people

Family size
number of children in an average family

one child

Years of life
number of years people can expect to live

represents 10 years

Work
if there were 100 people in the country, this is where they would work

farms   factories

offices and services

Rich and poor
the average amount each person spends in a year, converted into US dollars

$1000 $500

Health
the number of doctors for every 10 000 people

one doctor

Australia
7 741 000km²

20 100 000 people

1.7 children

80 years

$27 440

24 doctors

Bangladesh
144 000km²

141 300 000 people

3.3 children

60 years

$1700

2 doctors

Brazil
8 547 000km²

179 100 000 people

2.2 children

71 years

$7450

13 doctors

China
9 598 000km²

1 307 300 000 people

1.2 children

76 years

$4520

16 doctors

Ethiopia
1 104 000km²

72 400 000 people

5.9 children

46 years

$780

less than 1 doctor

© Oxford University Press

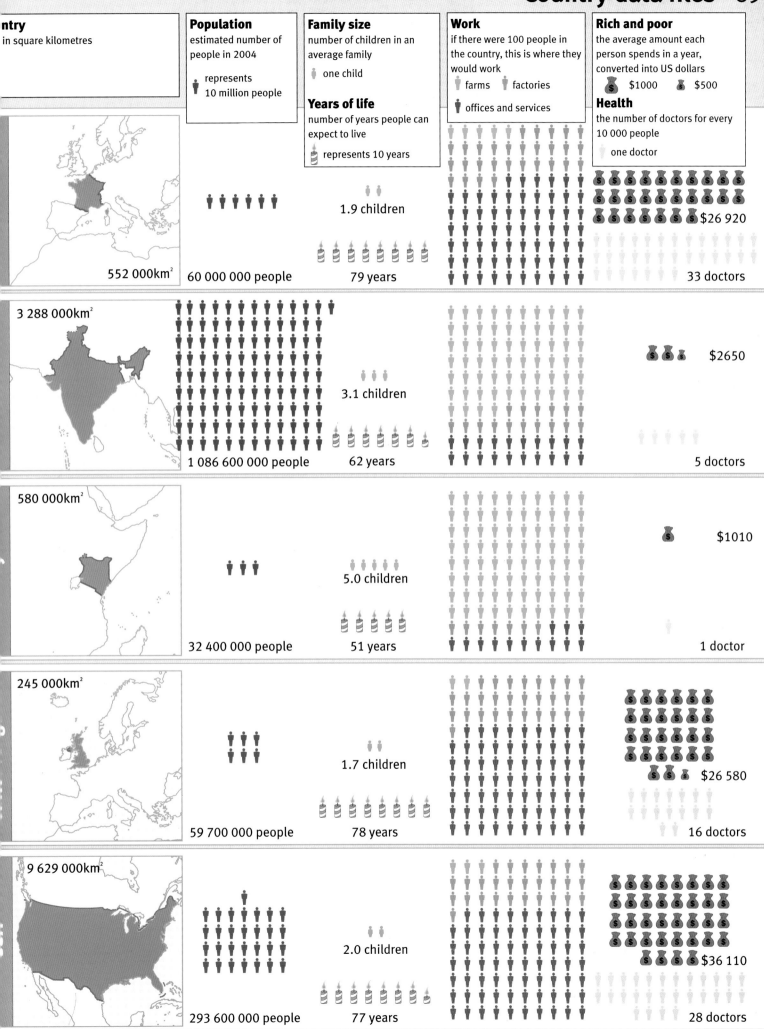

ntry
in square kilometres

Population
estimated number of people in 2004

represents 10 million people

Family size
number of children in an average family

one child

Years of life
number of years people can expect to live

represents 10 years

Work
if there were 100 people in the country, this is where they would work

farms   factories

offices and services

Rich and poor
the average amount each person spends in a year, converted into US dollars

$1000 $500

Health
the number of doctors for every 10 000 people

one doctor

---

552 000km²   60 000 000 people   1.9 children   79 years $26 920   33 doctors

3 288 000km²   1 086 600 000 people   3.1 children   62 years $2650   5 doctors

580 000km²   32 400 000 people   5.0 children   51 years $1010   1 doctor

245 000km²   59 700 000 people   1.7 children   78 years $26 580   16 doctors

9 629 000km²   293 600 000 people   2.0 children   77 years $36 110   28 doctors

70 Index

name of place   grid code

Leeds **15** F3

page number

A

Aberdeen **11** G2
Aberystwyth **14** C2
Abidjan **41** A4
Abu Dhabi **36** A3
Abuja **41** B4
Accra **41** A4
Aconcagua *mountain* **50** B2
Adana **33** G2
Addis Ababa **41** C4
Adelaide **54** B2
Aden, Gulf of **34** B3
Adriatic Sea **32/33** E3
Aegean Sea **33** F2
Afghanistan 35 C4
Ahmadabad **37** C3
Albania 33 E3/F3
Albany **54** A2
Aldabra Islands **41** D3
Aldeburgh **17** F3
Alderney *island* **19** E1
Aleppo **35** A4
Aleutian Islands **44** A3
Alexandria **42** B3
Algeria 41 A5/B5
Algiers **41** B5
Alice Springs *town* **54** B2
Alloa **13** E3
Almaty **35** C5
Alps *mountains* **32** D3
Alaska, Gulf of **44** B3
Altai Mountains **38** C4
Amazon, River **52/53** C4/D4
Amlwch **14** C3
Amman **35** A4
Amsterdam **32** D4
Amur, River **39** F5
Anatolian Plateau **30** D1
Anchorage **45** B4
Andaman Islands **37** E2
Andaman Sea **34** D3
Andes *mountains* **50** B1/B4
Andorra **32** D3
Angara River **34** D5/E5
Anglesey *island* **14** C3
Angola **41** B3/C3
Angola Plateau **40** B3
Anguilla **49** E2
Ankara **33** G2
Annan, River **13** E2
Antananarivo **41** D3
Antarctica **55**
Antigua and Barbuda 49 E2
Antofagasta **52** B2
Antrim **12** B1
Antrim Mountains **12** B1/B2
Appalachian Mountains **47** E2
Appennines *mountains* **32** E3
Arabian Peninsula **34** B4
Arabian Sea **36/37** B2
Arafura Sea **54** B3
Aral Sea **34** B5/C5
Ararat, Mount **30** E1
Arbroath **13** F3
Arctic Ocean **55**
Arequipa **52** B3
Argentina 51 B1/B2
Arkansas River **46/47** D2
Armagh **12** B1
Armenia 35 B5
Arnold **15** F2
Arran *island* **12** C2
Aruba **49** C1/D1
Arun, River **17** D2
Ascension Island **41** A3
Ashford **17** E2
Ashgabat **35** B4
Asmara **41** C4
Astana **35** C5
Asuncion **53** D2
Atacama Desert **52** B2/B3
Athens **33** F2
Atlanta **47** E2
Atlantic Ocean **30** B2
Atlas Mountains **40** A5/B5
Auckland **54** D2
Australia 54 A2/C3
Austria 32/33 E3
Aviemore **11** F2
Avon, River **15** F2
Ayers Rock *mountain* **54** B2
Aylesbury **17** D2
Ayr **12** D2
Azerbaijan 35 B5
Azov, Sea of **33** G3

B

Baffin Bay **44** F4/G4
Baffin Island **44** E4/F4
Baghdad **35** B4
Bahamas, The 48/49 B3/C3
Bahrain 35 B4
Baku **35** B5
Balearic Islands **32** D2/D3
Bali *island* **34** E2
Balkhash, Lake **34** C5
Ballybofey **12** A1
Ballymena **12** B1
Ballymoney **12** B2
Baltic Sea **32/33** E4
Bamako **41** A4
Banbridge **12** C1
Banbury **15** F2
Bandar Seri Begawan **35** E3
Bandung **35** E2
Bangalore **37** C2
Bangkok **35** E3
Bangladesh 37 D3/E3
Bangor Northern Ireland **12** C1
Bangor Wales **14** C3
Bangui **41** B4
Banjul **41** A4
Banks Island **44** C4/D4
Bann, River **12** B1
Barbados 49 F1
Barcelona **32** D3
Barents Sea **34** A6/B6
Barking **17** E2
Barmouth **14** C2
Barnet **17** D2
Barnstaple **18** C3
Barra *island* **10** B1/B2
Barranquilla **51** B4
Barrow-in-Furness **13** E1
Barrow, River **21**
Barry **14** D1
Basildon **17** E2
Basingstoke **19** F3
Basseterre **49** E2
Basse-Terre **49** E2
Bass Strait **54** C1/C2
Bath **19** E3
Baykal, Lake **34** E5
Beachy Head *cape* **17** E1
Beaufort Sea **44** B4/C4
Bedford **15** G2
Beijing **38** E3
Beira **41** C3
Beirut **35** A4
Belarus 33 F4
Belem **53** E4
Belfast **12** C1
Belfast Lough *estuary* **12** C1
Belgium 32 D4
Belgrade **33** F3
Belize 45 E1
Belmopan **45** E1
Belo Horizonte **53** E2
Benbecula *island* **10** B2
Ben Cruachan *mountain* **12** C3
Bengal, Bay of **37** D2/E2
Benghazi **41** C5
Benin 41 B4
Ben Nevis *mountain* **10** D1
Benue, River **40** B4
Ben Wyvis *mountain* **10** E2
Bering Sea **34** J5
Bering Strait **34** J6
Berlin **32** E4
Bermuda *island* **45** F2
Bern **32** D3
Berneray *island* **10** B2
Berwick-upon-Tweed **13** F2
Bexley **17** E2
Bhutan 37 D3/E3
Birkenhead **14** D3
Birmingham **15** F2
Biscay, Bay of **32** C3
Bishkek **35** C5
Bismarck Sea **54** C3
Bissau **41** A4
Blackburn **14** E3
Black Mountains **14** D1/D2
Blackpool **14** D3
Black Sea **33** G3
Blackwater, River **21**
Blue Nile River **40** C4
Blyth **13** G2
Bodmin Moor **18** C2
Bognor Regis **17** D1
Bogota **52** B5
Bolivia 52/53 D2
Bolton **14** E3
Bordeaux **32** C3
Borneo *island* **34** E2/E3
Bornholm *island* **32** E4
Bosnia-Herzegovina 33 E3
Boston UK **15** G2
Boston USA **47** F3
Bothnia, Gulf of **30** C3/D3
Botswana 41 C2
Bournemouth **19** F2
Boyne, River **21**

C

Bradford **15** F3
Braemar **11** F2
Brahmaputra River **37** E3
Brasilia **53** E3
Bratislava **33** E3
Brazil 52/53
Brazilian Highlands **53** E3
Brazzaville **41** B3
Brecon **14** D1
Brecon Beacons *mountains* **14** D1
Brent **17** D2
Bressay *island* **11** H5
Bridgend **14** D1
Bridgetown **49** F1
Bridgnorth **15** E2
Bridgwater **18** D3
Bridlington **13** H1
Brighton **17** D1
Brisbane **54** C2
Bristol **19** E3
Bristol Channel **18** C3/D3
Bromley **17** E2
Broome **54** B3
Brunei 35 E3
Brussels **32** D4
Bucharest **33** F3
Budapest **33** E3
Buenos Aires **51** C2
Bujumbura **41** C3
Bulgaria 33 F3
Bure, River **17** F3
Burkina 41 A4/B4
Burton upon Trent **15** F2
Bury **15** E3
Bury St. Edmunds **17** E3
Bute *island* **12** C2
Butt of Lewis *cape* **10** C3
Buxton **15** F3

C

Cabinda *admin.* **41** B3
Cadair Idris *mountain* **14** D2
Caernarfon **14** C3
Caerphilly **14** D1
Cairngorms *mountains* **11** F2
Cairns **54** C3
Cairo **42** C3
Calgary **45** D3
Cali **52** B5
California, Gulf of **44** E2/F3
Cambodia 35 E3
Cambrian Mountains **14** D2
Cambridge **17** E3
Cameroon 41 B4
Cameroun, Mount **40** B4
Campbeltown **12** C2
Canada 45 C4/G3
Canadian Shield **44** E3/F3
Canary Islands **41** A5
Canberra **54** C2
Canna *island* **10** C2
Cannock **15** E2
Cantabrian Mountains **32** C3
Canterbury **17** F2
Cape Town **41** B2
Cape Verde 56 D3
Cape York Peninsula **54** C3
Caracas **51** B4
Cardiff **14** D1
Cardigan **14** C2
Cardigan Bay **14** C2
Caribbean Sea **48/49**
Carlisle **13** F1
Carmarthen **14** C2
Carn Eige *mountain* **10** D2
Carpathians *mountains* **33** F3
Carpentaria, Gulf of **54** B3/C3
Carrickfergus **12** C1
Casablanca **41** A5
Caspian Sea **34** B4/B5
Castleblayney **12** B1
Castle Douglas **13** E1
Castleford **15** F3
Castries **49** G6
Caucasus *mountains* **30** E2
Cayenne **53** D4
Cayman Islands **48** A2/B2
Celebes Sea **34** E3/F3
Central African Republic 41 B4/C4
Central Russian Uplands **30** D2
Ceuta *territory* **32** C2
Chad 41 B4/C4
Chad, Lake **40** B4
Chang Jiang *river* **38** D2/D3
Channel Islands **19** E1
Chari, River **40** B4
Charlotte Amalie **49** E2
Chelmsford **17** E2
Cheltenham **16** B2
Chelyabinsk **35** C5
Chennai **37** D2
Cherwell, River **16** C2
Chester **14** E3
Chesterfield **15** F3
Cheviot Hills **13** F2
Chicago **47** E3

D

Chile 51 B1/B2
Chiloé Island **50** B1
Chiltern Hills **16/17** C2/D2
Chimborazo *mountain* **52** B4
China 35 D4/F5
Chisinau **33** F3
Chongqing **38** D2
Chorley **14** E3
Christchurch **54** D1
Cirencester **16** C2
Citlaltepetl *mountain* **44** E1
Clydebank **12** D2
Clyde, River **13** E2
Coalville **15** F2
Coast Mountains **44** C3
Cocos Islands **50** A4
Cod, Cape **47** G3
Colombia 51 B3/B4
Colombo **37** C1
Colonsay *island* **12** B3
Colorado Plateau **46** B2
Colorado, River Argentina **50** B2
Colorado River USA **46** B2
Columbia River **46** A3/B3
Colwyn Bay *town* **14** D3
Comoros 41 D3
Conakry **41** A4
Concepcion **51** B2
Congo 41 B3/B4
Congo, Democratic Republic of 41 B3/C4
Congo, River **40** C4
Consett **13** G1
Conwy **14** D3
Cook, Mount **54** D1
Cookstown **12** B1
Copenhagen **32** E4
Coquet, River **13** F2/G2
Coral Sea **54** C3
Corby **15** G2
Cordoba **53** C1
Corsica *island* **32** D3
Costa Rica 45 E1
Cote d'Ivoire **41** A4
Cotopaxi *mountain* **52** B4
Cotswold Hills **16** B2/C2
Coventry **15** F2
Crawley **17** D2
Crete *island* **33** F2
Crewe **14** E3
Croatia 32/33 E3
Cromer **17** F3
Croydon **17** D2
Cuba 48 A3/C3
Cubango, River **40** B3
Cuillin Hills **10** C2
Cumbernauld **13** E2
Cumnock **12** D2
Cunene, River **40** B3
Cunnamulla **54** C2
Curacao **49** D1
Curitiba **53** E2
Cwmbran **14** D1
Cyprus 33 G2
Czech Republic 32/33 E3/E4

D

Dakar **41** A4
Dalbeattie **13** E1
Dallas **47** D2
Damascus **35** B4
Danube, River **32/33** E3/F3
Dar es Salaam **41** C3
Darling, River **54** C2
Darlington **13** G1
Dartmoor **18** C2/D2
Dartmouth **18** D2
Dart, River **18** D2
Darwin **54** B3
Davis Strait **44** F4/G4
Dead Sea **34** A4
Deal **17** F2
Death Valley **46** B2
Deccan *plateau* **37** C2
Dee, River Scotland **11** G2
Dee, River Wales **14** D2/D3
Denbigh **14** D3
Denmark 32 D4/E4
Denmark Strait **44** H4
Denver **46** C2
Derby **15** F2
Derwent, River **15** F3
Detroit **47** E3
Deveron, River **11** G2
Devon Island **44** E4
Dhaka **37** E3
Dili **35** F2
Dinaric Alps *mountains* **33** E3
Dingwall **10** E2
Djibouti 41 D4
Djibouti **41** D4
Dniepr, River **33** G4
Dniester, River **33** F3
Dodoma **41** C3

E

Doha **35** B4
Dolgellau **14** D2
Dominica 49 E2
Dominican Republic 49 C2/D2
Doncaster **15** F3
Donets'k **33** G3
Donets, River **30** C2
Don, River England **15** F3
Don, River Russia **33** H3
Don, River Scotland **11** G2
Dorchester **19** E2
Dornoch Firth *estuary* **11** E2/F2
Douglas **12** C1
Dover **17** F2
Downpatrick **12** C1
Drakensberg *mountains* **40** C2
Dublin **32** C4
Dudley **15** E2
Duero, River **32** C3
Dumbarton **12** D2
Dumfries **13** E2
Duncansby Head *cape* **11** F3
Dundee **13** F3
Dunedin **54** D1
Dunfermline **13** E3
Dungannon **12** B1
Durban **41** C2
Durham **13** G1
Dushanbe **35** C4
Düsseldorf **32** D4
Dyfi, River **14** D2

E

Ealing **17** D2
Earn, River **13** E3
Eastbourne **17** E1
East China Sea **39** F2/F3
East Kilbride **12** D2
Eastleigh **19** F2
Ebro, River **32** C3
Ecuador 52 A4/B4
Eday *island* **11** G4
Eden, River **13** F1
Edinburgh **13** E2
Edmonton **45** D3
Egypt 42
Eigg *island* **10** C1
Elbe, River **32** E4
Elbrus, Mount **33** H3
Elburz Mountains **34** B4
Elgin **11** F2
El Giza **42** C2
Ellesmere Island **44** E4/F5
El Salvador 45 E1
Ely **17** E3
Emi Koussi *mountain* **40** B5
Enfield **17** D2
England 8/9
English Channel **32** C3/C4
Enniskillen **12** A1
Equatorial Guinea 41 B4
Erie, Lake **47** E3/F3
Eritrea 41 C4/D4
Esfahan **35** B4
Esk, River **13** E2
Espiritu Santo *island* **54** D3
Estonia 33 F4
Ethiopia 41 C4/D4
Ethiopian Highlands **40** C4
Etna, Mount **32** E2
Euphrates, River **34** B4
Everest, Mount **38** B2
Evesham **15** F2
Exe, River **18** D3
Exeter **18** D2
Exmoor **18** D3
Exmouth **18** D2
Eyre, Lake **54** B2

F

Fair Isle *island* **11** H4
Falkirk **13** E2
Falkland Islands **51** B1/C1
Falmouth **18** B2
Fareham **19** F2
Farewell, Cape **44** G4
Faroe Islands **30** B3
Federated States of Micronesia 57 H3
Felixstowe **17** F2
Fetlar *island* **11** J5
Fiji 57 H2
Finisterre, Cape **32** C3
Finland 31 D3
Firth of Clyde *estuary* **12** C2/D2
Firth of Forth *estuary* **13** E3/F3
Firth of Lorn *estuary* **12** C3
Fishguard **14** C1
Fitzroy, River **54** B3
Fleetwood **14** D3
Flinders, River **54** C2/C3
Folkestone **17** F2
Forel, Mount **44** H4
Forfar **13** F3
Fortaleza **53** F4
Fort Augustus **10** E2
Fort-de-France **49** E1

© Oxford University Press

World Flags

 Afghanistan
 Albania
 Algeria
 Andorra
 Angola
 Antigua and Barbuda
 Argentina

 Armenia
 Australia
 Austria
 Azerbaijan
 Bahamas
 Bahrain
 Bangladesh

 Barbados
 Belarus
 Belgium
 Belize
 Benin
 Bhutan
 Bolivia

 Bosnia-Herzegovina
 Botswana
 Brazil
 Brunei
 Bulgaria
 Burkina
 Burundi

 Cambodia
 Cameroon
 Canada
 Cape Verde
 Central African Republic
 Chad
 Chile

 China
 Colombia
 Comoros
 Congo
 Congo, Dem. Rep.
 Costa Rica
 Côte d'Ivoire

 Croatia
 Cuba
 Cyprus
 Czech Republic
 Denmark
 Djibouti
 Dominica

 Dominican Republic
 East Timor
 Ecuador
 Egypt
 El Salvador
 Equatorial Guinea
 Eritrea

 Estonia
 Ethiopia
 Fiji
 Finland
 France
 French Guiana
 Gabon

 Gambia
 Georgia
 Germany
 Ghana
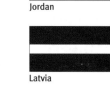 Greece
 Greenland
 Grenada

 Guatemala
 Guinea
 Guinea-Bissau
 Guyana
 Haiti
 Honduras
 Hungary

 Iceland
 India
 Indonesia
 Iran
 Iraq
Ireland
Israel

Italy
Jamaica
Japan
Jordan
Kazakhstan
Kenya
Kiribati

Kuwait
Kyrgyzstan
Laos
Latvia
Lebanon
Lesotho
Liberia